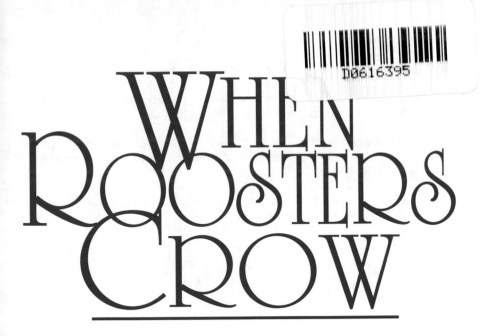

WHEN ROOSTERS CROW

By Lori Salierno

with Esther M. Bailey

WARNER PRESS
ANDERSON, INDIANA

Copyright © 1997 by Warner Press, Inc
ISBN 0-87162-813-9

All Rights Reserved
Printed in the United States of America
Warner Press, Inc

David C. Shultz, Editor in Chief
Arthur Kelly, Managing Editor
C. Richard Craghead, Editor
Cover and Layout by
   Curtis D. Corzine and Virginia L. Wachenschwanz

Erma,
Celebrate Jesus!

Lori Salierno
Rom 12:11

To my dear roosters—

Thank you for the love, support, prayer, and biblical accountability that you have given to me. Your influence has made a difference in my ministry. To you I dedicate this book.

THE ROOSTERS OF PHOENIX

> Judy Birt
> Lori Brown
> Janet Egelston
> Nova Forrest
> Elaine Hansen
> Donna McBroom
> Pam Osborne

THE ROOSTERS OF ATLANTA

> Michelle Crose
> Suzanne Davenport
> Cheri Harp
> Julie Hunker
> Shelli Lahmann
> Lisa Maldonado
> Robyn Smith
> Wanza Walston

Contents

FOREWORD

I first met Lori in 1993 when she attended my C.L.A.S.S. seminar. Four years later she is an accomplished author and communicator. Lori's ministry has reached literally thousands of people in both the Christian and secular arenas. Her platform includes universities, public high shcools, leadership training conferences, women's retreats, and youth conventions.

If there is one word to describe Lori's message it is enthusiastic. She's the kind of person who rents a Corvette for a date night with her husband, jumps out of an airplane at 18,000 feet, and climbs Mount Kilimanjaro for adventure. She brings that same spirit of adventure to the tasks of leadership and accountability. Applicable to both the church and the secular world, *When Roosters Crow* will equip youth leaders, pastors, board members, laymen, and business persons alike.

With penetrating wisdom Lori has entered our private world and addressed an issue of great concern—our need for accountability. With leadership training experience nationwide and in the local church, Lori has earned the right to be heard. Through personal stories and the experience of others, she brings biblical truths of accountability to life.

When Roosters Crow is not a theoretical textbook; it is a resource for leaders that offers practical and experienced guidance on how Christian leaders can protect themselves from situations that are loaded with temptations and seduction. You will be given a step-by-step strategy for identifying, selecting, recruiting, and training a team of persons who will surround your ministry with support. Her fresh approach and creative style bring a dynamic dimension to leadership. Best of all, Lori models her message as well as she communicates it. With much enthusiasm I recommend this book to any leader who desires integrity in every area of his or her work or ministry.

Florence Littauer
Popular author, speaker, and founder of C.L.A.S.S.
(Christian Leaders, Authors, & Speakers Seminar)

PREFACE

When I speak to students or conduct conferences for various organizations, I often schedule appointments with individuals. Through my one-on-one ministry I catch a glimpse of trends in the church community. Sometimes I am encouraged by those who seek to maintain a fresh relationship with the Lord. At other times I am appalled by the lack of integrity in professing Christians, particularly those involved in leadership.

During one of my speaking engagements a key leader made an appointment with me. I'll refer to him as Dr. Carlson to indicate his status in the community. The thirty-three-year-old man told me a story of a life tainted by addiction to pornography.

I concealed my shock and interrupted his speaking to avoid hearing more. "Sir, I need to make a statement, and I hope you understand I do so with compassion. But, sir, you're sick."

The turmoil that churned in his soul showed on his face. He spoke softly, "I know I am."

"Does anyone in your life know about this?"

"Well, my wife knows I struggle with … girls."

Somehow I sensed his problem went even deeper. "Struggle? Or are you actually involved?"

He sighed. "If my wife knew the extent of what I've just told you, I would not have a wife.

The situation called for shock treatment, and I breathed a prayer for direction. At that moment a question once posed by John Maxwell popped into my mind. "You know what? You need a rooster," I said.

"What?"

"You need a rooster."

"What does a rooster have to do with my problem?"

I tried to direct Dr. Carlson's mind away from an adult bookstore and toward the high priest's residence where Jesus was taken after his arrest. The Apostle Peter followed in the shadows as Jesus was moved from one temple leader to another. Each time Peter was asked whether he was one of the disciples of Jesus, he denied the connection and widened the distance between himself and his Lord. After the third denial a cock crowed, calling Peter to accountability for his failure (John 18:15–27). I wanted Dr. Carlson to look into the face of Jesus with Peter and see the pain on the Savior's face. The rooster's call would require Dr. Carlson to "[renounce] the shameful things that one hides" (2 Cor 4:2). Repeating the question asked by my pastor, I asked, "Who is your rooster?"

His spirit broken, Dr. Carlson choked back tears as he whispered, "How do I find one?" My time schedule did not permit me to give him an adequate answer.

I began to place more emphasis on the theme of accountability in my talks. After my address to seven hundred executive directors of an international Christian organization, people lined up to ask questions. Most of the questions dealt with the issue of accountability.

During the parting conversation with my hostess, she said, "If you did anything that touched our leaders, it was in the area of accountability. We haven't been taught that concept, and we have no system to help us stay fresh and effective in ministry."

So it is that I say to Dr. Carlson, seven hundred executive directors, and everyone from aspiring leaders to those who have reached the top, "Find yourself a rooster." A rooster represents a signal sent from God to warn you when your soul is in danger. With your cooperation the Holy Spirit can work to preserve integrity and spiritual vitality that will last a lifetime.

This book draws on the Bible, conventional wisdom, the principles and practices of ethical behavior taught in the church at large, and personal experiences of many people, myself included. Each chapter recounts conversations I have had with Christian leaders who have struggled to recover or retain integrity that grows from a close relationship with God in Christ.

A veteran minister told me that in his experience forty or fifty years ago, considerable emphasis was placed on the training of young ministers to be accountable to God. "In fact," he said, "I was given lopsided advice that said I was not accountable to people in the church community, only to God who had called me to ministry."

He lamented that he had confined God's self-revelation to only a few channels, primarily those having to do with inner convictions. He said he wished that he had known more about "roosters" in the first five years of his ministry when he gave very little thought to those who could have helped him with his work for God. Even so, he admitted that he often played the role of a "rooster" by telling others how to conduct themselves, whether or not they invited such advice.

You will find this to be a practical book and a challenge to your spiritual growth. I encourage you to take time with the Reader Challenge at the end of each chapter. Do as many of the strategies as you can find time to do. I follow these disciplines myself and find my life and ministry the richer for it.

Let me encourage you to stay with this book until you get to the final chapter on the risks of leadership. You don't have to stumble and fall over issues that have tripped up many well-meaning but unwary Christian leaders.

—Lori Salierno
Spring, 1997

CHAPTER 1

Signals from Scripture

Throughout the Bible we find various examples of signals God used to warn people who needed divine direction. In the Old Testament God caught the attention of Moses through a burning bush and a slithering snake (Exod 3—4). A talking donkey led by an angel cautioned Balaam to listen for God's voice in dealing with the king of Moab (Num 22—24).

In the New Testament Jesus revealed himself to Saul of Tarsus with a blinding light from heaven (Acts 9). A vision of a sheet suspended in the air filled with living creatures restricted from the Jewish diet gave Peter a two-fold message: God lifted the taboos against certain foods and welcomed Gentiles into the church (Acts 10).

More often than not God confronted the wayward ones through people—namely the prophets under the Law and the apostles under the new covenant. For instance, in dramatic fashion Nathan the prophet used a parable to compel King David to recognize his sin against Uriah (2 Sam 12). David's anger mounted as he listened to the story he believed to be true: To feed a guest, a rich man with a vast number of sheep and cattle had slaughtered the pet lamb of a poor man who owned no other animals.

"That man deserves death!" David impetuously exclaimed, and then he proceeded to specify the offender's punishment.

Before David could issue an order, Nathan looked squarely into the king's eyes and declared, "You are the man."

David clearly understood the teaching of the parable: He himself was guilty of adultery and murder. Not only had David impregnated Uriah's wife, Bathsheba, but he then arranged for Uriah to be killed in battle to conceal his sin.

Today we have benefit of all the warnings contained in Scripture. With the Holy Spirit acting as our interpreter, we can extract practical value from biblical examples.

The Rooster's Wake-up Call

When I was a young teen, I didn't make the connection between crowing and warning signals, but I can look back now and almost hear with Peter the echo of the rooster's wake-up call. During my junior high years my inborn independent spirit took the form of open rebellion. Although I recognized God's authority, I thought I was qualified to run my own life without help from anyone else, especially my parents.

One day when my mother was ready to give up on me, my father took charge. It would have been easier to deal with Mom than to follow through with Dad's ultimatum, but I had no choice. He was going to make a pastoral visit, and I was going along. Period! First, though, I had to make a card to take to Mrs. Stalnaker.

"Be ready in half an hour," Dad said.

Well—it wouldn't take me that long. At least I could show my defiance in the quality of art work I produced. I snatched the sheet of construction paper from Dad's hand and went to my room. After deliberately folding the paper so the edges were uneven, I ripped a flower from a magazine and pasted it on the front of the card. Inside I wrote, "I love you. Lori."

The words I wrote had no real meaning. Mrs. Stalnaker was practically a nonperson to me. Any time I saw her in her wheelchair at church, I spoke to her but felt no emotion in the exchange of greetings.

As soon as Dad and I got to Mrs. Stalnaker's house, I handed her the card to get my assignment over with as quickly as possible. I was totally unprepared for her reaction.

With tears streaming down her face, the invalid lady said, "You are such a blessing. You are the sweetest girl I know."

My remorse could not have been greater had I heard the crowing of the rooster and looked into the disappointed face of Jesus. At that moment I knew my attitude had to change if I wanted to be an effective witness for Christ.

The Formative Years

Another lady in the church played an important role in my life. In helping me explore the positive and negative aspects of various careers, Minna Jarrett influenced me in much the same way as Eli the priest guided Samuel (1 Sam 3).

Although retired by the time I knew her, Sister Jarrett had had an interesting career built around the church. The church my dad pastored in Vancouver, Washington was started through her labor. In eighth grade I aspired to be a reporter, and so I decided to interview Sister Jarrett.

Listening to the tapes I made then makes me feel ridiculous now. My teen version of professionalism was overdone, but the gracious lady answered my questions as seriously as if I'd been a top reporter with NBC.

When I finished recording Sister Jarrett's life story after several visits, she inquired, "Tell me, Lori, what do you want to do with your life?"

By then my ambition had changed. "I'm going to be an actress and go to Hollywood."

"That's very interesting." For a moment Sister Jarrett was silent as if in deep thought. Then she spoke gently. "If you become an actress, can you still serve the Lord?"

"Oh, yes! No question about it. I'll play in Christian movies and lead people to Jesus Christ."

Nodding her wise head, she said, "That's wonderful, but be very careful. People who go to Hollywood often change. It's easy to get caught up in seeking personal glory."

A few months later I told Sister Jarrett I wanted to become a psychiatrist. Again she came through with solid advice. "Lori, be very careful," she said. "People who give out help often end up needing the same kind of help themselves."

I was a junior in high school when I told my loyal friend I felt called to the ministry. Other people had discouraged me, but Sister Jarrett said, "Go for it!"

Three or four years later my dad arranged my first speaking engagement. Spotting Sister Jarrett's friendly face in the audience boosted my confidence. Afterward, she took me by the shoulders and said, "I have no doubts. You are indeed gifted by God and called to the ministry." Her affirmation carried me through many rough times ahead.

The Mantle

When I think about the mentors who have helped me along life's journey, Dr. Marie Strong always comes to my mind. I like to compare her influence on my ministry to that of Elijah's role in Elisha's life (2 Kings 2). While I don't claim to inherit a double portion of Dr. Strong's spirit, I do believe her mantle touched my life.

As a new student in her class, I did not expect Dr. Strong to play an important role in my life. While I

recognized her as a good Bible professor, her somewhat austere manner made me uncomfortable. When she requested I stay after class, I became even more uncomfortable.

"You have a problem I want corrected in my class," she said.

"What's that?"

"You're consistently late."

"Only two or three minutes," I said.

"Late is late. I want you here on time. Do you have a problem with that?"

Could she actually be that inflexible? I wondered. Daring to test her I said, "I don't think I can do it."

"You *will* do it. From now on I'll expect you here on time."

That did it! If she was that tyrannical after only a couple of weeks, what would she be like by the semester's end? In my heart I vowed to drop her class.

While my mind entertained such thoughts, Professor Strong flashed me a rare smile. "I have good news, too."

Good news always sparks my interest. Perhaps I had been too hasty in judging the professor. I waited eagerly for her next words.

"If you will apply yourself," she said, "you will receive the highest grade in this class, and you will go farther than any of the other students."

Shocked, I said, "How do you know that?"

"Because I know you. You're dismissed."

From that day forward I arrived early to class, sat on the front row, and got the highest grade on every test. By the end of the semester Dr. Strong looked beautiful to me, and I decided to take every course she taught.

One of the highlights of my college years happened the day Professor Strong invited me to lunch. I anticipated an interesting conversation, and she did not let me down. As Dr. Strong described what she saw as my potential, I set my sights on bigger things than ever before. Many of the goals we talked about that day have come to pass, and part of the credit belongs to Dr. Marie Strong because she believed in me.

Self-imposed Discipline

Although I tend to resist following rules dictated by others, I can be quite rigid in demands I make of myself. After attending a seminar on prayer I decided to spend an hour a day praying and reading the Bible. Like the Apostle Paul I was determined to "punish my body and enslave it, so that after proclaiming to others I myself should not be disqualified" (1 Cor 9:27).

During a four-year period from mid-high school to mid-college I held to a rigid schedule. Nothing could keep me from my hour of power. The problem was that my devotions turned into an obsession to follow a

ritual instead of an act of worship. When I made comments such as, "So-and-so must not be a very good Christian. She doesn't even have regular devotions," my dad got concerned.

"Lori, you're getting too legalistic," Dad said. "I want you to go four days without opening your Bible or spending time in prayer."

"But, Dad, I don't think I'd even feel saved if I did that," I protested.

"That's just the point. You're basing salvation on works rather than on God's grace. Take a break for four days, loosen up, and just let God love you. Your prayer time will actually become richer if it's less regimented."

For four days my Bible lay closed, and I thought I'd go to hell for sure. I couldn't quite give up my prayer time, although I did change my routine. Instead of bowing before the Lord, I prayed on the run while walking, biking, or listening to inspirational music.

When I started dating Kurt Salierno in college, he helped me understand God's grace more clearly. "You're like a Pharisee," he said. "You follow all the rules, but are you loving people?"

Remembering how Jesus condemned the Pharisees, I knew I could never be effective in ministry with that kind of an attitude.

Of course I didn't need to change *what* I did; I just needed to change why I did it. The Pharisees did right in giving a tenth of their income to God. Jesus told them they should continue to tithe, but the motive from their hearts should be governed by love and justice (Luke 11:42). In my case I needed to eradicate my harsh judgment of others who failed to follow my example.

Even though my devotional life was less than ideal during those four years of college, I believe God honored my faithfulness. The insight I gained from Scripture continues to have value for me today, especially those passages committed to memory.

A daily quiet time with the Lord still ranks number one on my priority list, but I count it a privilege rather than a duty. God *desires* to communicate with me. That fact alone permeates every atom of my being with wonder. Equally important, though, is my *need* to talk to God about everything that goes on in my life. I conclude prayer times with joy surging through my soul.

Biblical Burnout

While attending graduate school, I encountered a problem common to Christian leaders. Some of my assignments to write lengthy papers required me to spend several hours a day with the Bible. For advice I called my former college professor, Dr. Marie Strong, who had become a close friend by then.

"I'm having trouble doing my personal devotions," I said. "By the time I finish studying, I'm sick of the Bible. Is that bad or what?"

"No," she said, and I began to breathe easier. "What you need to do is invite God into your study time. Focus your mind on a particular verse of Scripture, stop and say, 'Lord, this is a rich thought. May it edify my life so I can help others.' As God becomes part of your process, you might end up doing devotions for six hours a day."

That was a tremendous concept that has often helped me deal with a hectic schedule. At other times, though, I like to turn off the message I'm preparing for others. I sometimes open my Bible and ask God for a fresh anointing meant specifically for me and me alone.

To me, variety is the key to pulling personal signals from God's Word. As I read the Psalms, I can either join in praise to almighty God or unite with the psalmist to pray for God's help in times of discouragement. When I'm wrestling with a problem, I might claim a particular verse of Scripture as God's promise to me. Listening to tapes of old hymns that carry a biblical message soothes my spirit after a trying day. Creativity in worship helps me prevent the kind of burnout that comes from repeating a particular procedure until boredom sets in.

Stored Signals

Scripture stored in memory becomes a permanent resource available for instruction and correction. The psalmist wrote, "I have hidden your word in my heart that I might not sin against you" (Ps 119:11, NIV).

When I'm disturbed about something, I pull a related biblical passage from memory and replay it over and over in my mind. As I stay tuned to God's voice, I tend to keep a more spiritual focus.

The different versions and paraphrases of the Bible provide excellent help for in-depth study, but they play havoc with memorization. For the most part I memorize from only one version to avoid confusion. Unless I want to preserve a particularly beautiful expression, I avoid paraphrases because the authors are using their own words instead of translating the original manuscript.

For many years the New International Version (NIV) has been my favorite source of Scripture. When a passage calls for inclusive language, however, the New Revised Standard Version (NRSV) is preferable.

Sometimes a verse of Scripture strikes me with such force that I can instantly recall every word of the text. When that happens I make it a point to memorize the reference. Just as I can't direct anyone to the church without an address, I can't recommend a verse to meet someone's need without the biblical reference. To reinforce my memory I repeat the reference before and after the text each time I quote the verse. For example: "2 Timothy 2:15, 'Do your best to present yourself to God as one approved, a workman who does not need to be ashamed and who correctly handles the word of truth.' 2 Timothy 2:15."

As the premier accountability partner, the Bible provides a variety of signals to keep us on track spiritually. In fact, all other forms of accountability must be measured against the Bible for authenticity. Human counsel can be beneficial if it corroborates Scripture. Any advice that contradicts Scripture must be rejected no matter how wise it may seem.

Reader Challenge

• As you think about this chapter do you hear the echo of a crowing rooster telling you where you have failed your Lord? What does the rooster say to you? If all is silent, will you take a moment to ask God what voice you should hear? How will you respond to that voice?

• Do you see a parallel between Eli the priest and someone in your life? Is anyone helping you find your place in the kingdom of God? Are you listening for God's voice through that person? If you have no one in your life acting as a priest, will you ask God for someone to fill that role?

• Has God sent an Elijah into your life? Are you ready for God to inspire you with the spirit of a godly leader?

• Do you maintain a consistent devotional life? Is your time with the Lord a privilege or a duty? How can you be more creative in your private worship?

• If all the Bibles in the land were confiscated, could you quote enough Scripture to nourish your faith? No matter how much Scripture you already know, will you make a regular effort to increase your store of knowledge?

• From these questions, choose the one that challenges you to action. Write out the steps you will take to increase the value you receive from God's Word.

• Rephrase the following prayer in your own words:

ALMIGHTY GOD, thank you for calling me to accountability through the holy Scriptures. Thank you for the Holy Spirit who translates yesterday's inspiration into an answer for today's dilemma. Help me to be sensitive to your voice and to respond to divine direction. In Jesus' name I pray. Amen.

CHAPTER 2
Intentional Accountability

After building a temple to the Lord, King Solomon built a wall around the city of Jerusalem to protect the place of worship (1 Kings 9:15). Later in history, God put it into the heart of Nehemiah to rebuild the wall which had been destroyed during the Babylonian captivity (Neh 2:12). In each instance, protection resulted from the human and divine working together.

As temples of God, we need to take the initiative to protect ourselves from Satan's attacks. Scripture tells us how to form protective walls around ourselves. "Without counsel, plans go wrong, but with many advisers they succeed" (Prov 15:22). "Two are better than one.... For if they fall, one will lift up the other; but woe to one who is alone and falls and does not have another to help" (Eccles 4:9–10).

Persons we enlist to help us keep our ministry on track function in much the same way as the offensive linemen on a football team. If the quarterback makes a successful play, it is likely because of the protection of the linemen.

The idea of being accountable to others makes some people nervous. They feel their reputation is threatened if anyone suggests a system of checks and balances. That is how the treasurer of one church felt when the board of trustees voted to have a yearly audit of the books. Rather than be subject to scrutiny, the treasurer resigned and left the church.

In contrast, a lady in another church became concerned when the board over her ceased to function. The bylaws called for an appointment to her position every year. "I feel I'm operating unofficially," she said. "It bothers me that I'm accountable to no one." If anyone was ever above the need for supervision, this godly woman was, but she would have preferred to include others in the decision-making process.

Taking intentional steps to become accountable is a sign of strength, not weakness. We consider our ministry and our relationship with the Lord too precious to take lightly. "Let the wise also hear and gain in learning, and the discerning acquire skill" (Prov 1:5).

Along with the value of accountability, we must also consider the dangers. Even well-intentioned accountability can go sour.

Risk Factors

The story has been told about three preachers named Mike, Joe, and Harry. One Saturday morning the three men decided to take a break from parish duties to go fishing. As they got in the boat and drove out on the lake, they anticipated a great day. For a while they enjoyed the perfect weather and solitude, even though they weren't catching any fish. After a couple of hours, the men began to get bored.

"I should have stayed home to put some finishing touches on my sermon," Joe said.

Mike still hoped for a miracle. "Wouldn't it be great if we could tell the story about the miraculous catch of fish from personal experience?" he mused.

"I don't have that much faith, but I have an idea," Harry said. "Why don't we confess our faults to each other? It would be good for our souls. In fact, I'll go first. I've been counseling with a couple of ladies in my congregation and … well, I wouldn't want my wife to know how I feel about them."

"Since you led the way, I guess I'll confess, too," Joe said. "As you know, our church doesn't condemn moderate drinking, but I've been known to sneak a few extra drinks, and now it's beginning to get out of hand."

Mike remained silent. The other two men waited for him to speak, but Mike decided it was time to try another bait. Finally, Joe prompted, "Come on, Mike. You must have something to tell us."

"I don't feel comfortable relating my weakness."

"It will be good for you. I feel better already for admitting I'm attracted to the ladies," Harry said. "Besides, the Apostle James tells us to confess our sins and pray for each other."

"Well," Mike said, "my problem is gossip, and I can't wait to get back on land."

In real life, a similar situation loses the humor that can be incorporated into make-believe. After one of my seminars where I emphasized the need for accountability, a pastor's wife came up to me with tears in her eyes. "What do you do if you opened up to someone who betrayed your trust?"

My heart ached for the woman because I have known others who have been hurt. I placed my arm on her shoulder. "First, don't let a bad experience rob you of the value of accountability," I said. Then I briefly discussed how I select an accountability partner.

Profile of a Confidant

If we base our selection process on the calling of Christ's disciples, we will not expect to find perfect people. Jesus was perfect, but his support people were not.

As a tax collector, Matthew did nothing to enhance the popularity of Jesus. Even if Matthew had conducted his business according to ethical standards, he would have been perceived as a ruthless bureaucrat like others who increased taxes and pocketed the difference. Besides, the Jews considered anyone aligned with Rome to be a traitor.

Peter, referred to as the Rock, sometimes behaved like Peter the Pebble. Nevertheless, this impetuous man, a mixture of courage and cowardice, left us a spiritual legacy—including how to handle failure.

Of course, Judas Iscariot may have been Christ's biggest disappointment. Yet even in his betrayal, Judas provided a measure of hope to Christian leaders who lean on others. If Jesus' ministry survived the setback inflicted by Judas (and it did), our ministry can continue even after someone betrays our confidence. The resurrection of Jesus proves that we can rise above any damage done by someone who violates a trust.

Even though we shouldn't expect always to find "perfect" people, we will want to exercise extreme caution in choosing those who will participate in our ministry. I consider the first criterion to be a fervent commitment to Jesus Christ that extends beyond the church walls. "Let the righteous strike me; let the faithful correct me" (Ps 141:5). Only godly people with a consistent Christian lifestyle qualify. That means living the gospel at home, at work, and at play.

While I appreciate all the prayers I can get, I look for team members who are interested in my particular ministry. Someone who is concerned mainly about the elderly will not relate as well with my focus on youth.

Of course, I find some people who wish to broaden their scope of interest, and I'm pleased to provide that opportunity.

The ability to keep secrets is an essential quality for those who would serve in partnership with leaders. I actually have two groups working with me—a large group of prayer warriors to support me when I'm on the road and a core group to help me deal with more intimate details. Especially in the core group I look for those who can be trusted with confidential material.

The Prayer Warriors

When I first started to take my ministry on the road, I asked a few close friends and family members to pray for me during my travel time and speaking engagements. Although my ministry got off to a good start, I soon felt the need for more of the power that comes through prayer.

Satan enjoys a stronghold in schools and universities, and he declares all-out warfare any time his position is threatened. Only through the power of the Holy Spirit, released during fervent prayer, can we defeat the devil.

As names of people who might help me battle the enemy came to mind, I wrote letters inviting their participation and requested a reply in writing if they wanted to support me for a specified period—usually a year. Somehow a written commitment is more binding than one made verbally. Also, the indirect approach allowed individuals more freedom to decline if they so chose.

At this time two hundred fifty people comprise my list of prayer warriors. To me they are like the seventy leaders Jesus appointed to go ahead of him into the towns he intended to visit (Luke 10). My prayer warriors received a copy of my schedule, and I asked them to cover me with prayer from the time I left home until my return.

Almost immediately, dramatic results began to take place. When I arrived at one college, the chaplain was extremely distraught because a woman on campus had been raped by her date the night before. He asked me to speak to the student body about sexuality.

After my talk I went to the women's dorm for further discussion. The tough questions asked by the girls challenged me to depend on the Holy Spirit as never before. Within myself I had no easy answers to restore wholeness to women whose lives had been broken. At the close of the last chapel service more than one hundred students and many faculty members bowed at the altar to receive healing that only God can bring.

In some situations I have made long-distance calls to ask the prayer warriors to go into battle against the forces of evil. Especially in public schools I sometimes encounter a hostile environment.

One high school principal communicated his displeasure quite effectively. "I don't know how you got scheduled to speak here," he said. "Now that you're here, we'll let you speak, but are you aware of the line between church and state?"

"Yes, sir, I am."

"What are you going to speak about?"

"Making wise choices."

"Do you promote safe sex?"

"No, sir, I take the position of abstinence."

His expression indicated he was losing patience. "I won't be responsible for how the students receive you," he said. "They may jeer you or walk out on you, and I won't try to stop them. You're on your own." Well, not exactly, but he had no way of knowing God was on my side.

Almost as soon as I began to speak, I held the attention of the students, but their interest intensified as my talk progressed. When I finished the principal said, "I'm amazed. Not only did they listen to you, they even considered your message might have merit. How did you do it?"

Taking my cue from Jesus (Luke 20:8) I said, "I can't tell you. It would violate the line between church and state."

When Christian faculty members ask for the secret of effective ministry, I tell them about my prayer warriors. If my talks cause students to commit their lives to Christ or pledge to stay sexually pure or decide to go into full-time ministry, I know it is the result of people who pray for me.

The Safety Factor

In addition to interceding with God on behalf of my ministry, the prayer warriors also pray for my personal protection. As my trusting nature is exposed to the reality of danger, I become more appreciative of the value of this kind of support.

During one of my engagements a lady became concerned about my safety to the point she felt compelled to contact me. My agent hesitated to give out information on where I was speaking. Not willing to give up, my prayer warrior insisted she was calling about an emergency.

When the lady finally reached my host university, the person answering the phone did not want to put her through to me. Again, her persistence prevailed.

About the same time the woman received the premonition, I had slipped away to a secluded spot on campus to enjoy quiet time with the Lord. One moment I was totally relaxed, and the next moment I felt an urge to return to my room.

I got back just as the call was coming through. "Have you been alone today?" My prayer warrior's voice revealed her anxiety.

"Yes, I just came in."

"Don't go off by yourself again. My impression that you might be in danger was so strong I just had to warn you."

The incident reminded me of some of my husband's experiences before we were married. While in college Kurt ministered to the derelicts of skid row in Portland, Oregon.[1] Life on the streets represented real danger as well as opportunities to share the gospel.

Before periodically leaving college to sleep and eat with the vagrants, Kurt arranged for prayer support from his roommates and two families. During the two and a half years of his ministry, Kurt was threatened, assaulted, shot at, and nearly captured by two drunks who bragged they would kill him. As he prayed during each crisis, Kurt took comfort in knowing others were praying with him.

On one occasion Kurt felt God was directing him to undertake a risky venture. Unwilling to trust his own instincts, Kurt walked the sixteen miles to campus to counsel with his prayer warriors. After hearing Kurt out, they agreed his impression came from God. One of the men gave Kurt enough money for a round-trip bus ticket. Assured that his friends would be praying, Kurt returned to the streets to accomplish the task assigned by God.

Looking back now, I wonder what might have happened if people had not prayed for Kurt, or a woman in North Dakota had not prayed for me. In any event, I am learning to appreciate God's warning signals as a safety factor.

My Core Group

On several occasions Jesus singled out three of his disciples as a support team. Peter, James, and John accompanied Jesus to the mountain where the transfiguration took place. Only those three men were present when Jesus raised the daughter of Jairus from

the dead. In Gethsemane, though, they slept when Jesus needed them most.

For the last year I lived in Phoenix six women formed my core group. We held weekly meetings and were mutually accountable to each other. Each person kept a daily record of progress in specified areas. Sometimes we shared reports with the entire group. At other times we split up into two or three groups.

• Use the sample form to make up your own accountability sheets:

ACCOUNTABILITY SHEET

Date: _____

Scripture Reference: _____

Application of Scripture: _____

_____

Scripture Memory: _____

Exercise: Yes ___ No ___

Habits:
      Gossip   Yes ___ No ___
      Criticism   Yes ___ No ___
      Foul Language   Yes ___ No ___

Relationships: Good   Fair   Poor
      Spouse   _____   _____   _____
      Friends   _____   _____   _____
      Children   _____   _____   _____
      Co-worker   _____   _____   _____

I make up weekly accountability sheets, placing forms for Monday through Thursday on the front and Friday through Sunday on the back. That leaves one page for comments on the back to be filled in by the person receiving the sheet.

Depending on the needs of the group, I sometimes ask participants for more detailed information. I may ask for specific times when they began and ended Bible study, exercise, or even sleep. Calling for a two to three sentence statement of application on Scripture brings the Bible to life for group members.

Choosing individuals who will share intimate secrets requires the utmost care. Although I seldom choose close friends, because they tend to be less objective, I usually favor people I know well. Trust builds over a period of time. As a test, I might pass on a bit of confidential but innocuous information to see if it comes back to me. After two or three experiences with no feedback, I consider the individual to be a good candidate for a long-term relationship.

I change accountability partners every year or so. The strong bonds that develop within an accountability group sometimes create a feeling of "ownership" that stifles individual freedom. Without meaning to, an accountability partner can become so possessive that she does not want to relinquish control. Setting a time limit in the beginning will avoid misunderstanding later.

When I first met with the women in Phoenix, we decided to call ourselves The Joy Team. In the beginning we established guidelines so everyone knew what was expected. The covenant we signed required strict confidentiality except with permission of everyone involved. So our husbands would not feel left out, we agreed on which information to share with them and which to keep private.

Covenant to serve on *THE JOY TEAM*

To the best of my ability I commit to serve on *The Joy Team* during the next year. I agree to spend time in prayer and reading the Bible on a daily basis, and to record my spiritual progress each day on a weekly accountability sheet, which has been provided. Instead of excusing or glossing over my failures, I will honestly admit my faults and make an effort to correct them. To be an example to others, I will not partake of drugs or alcohol during the time this covenant is in effect.

Unless an emergency arises, I will faithfully attend meetings on a weekly basis.

Furthermore, I promise to keep confidential everything revealed by any member of the group.

_____
Signature

Some of the experiences of women in the group provide good illustrations to encourage others. With their permission I relate these anecdotes anonymously in my talks and in this book. Their stories will appear in the chapters where their experiences offer insight. For now, I will briefly introduce the women with fictitious names they have chosen.

"Kayleen"

When I invited Kayleen to become part of my group, she hesitated. "I—I'm just a new Christian and don't know much about the Bible," she said.

"I know, Kayleen, and that's exactly why I want you," I said. "You're not 'churchy,' so you know how unchurched people think. You can teach me how to reach them." Although I saw a need for this kind of help, I had no idea then how much Kayleen would contribute to my ministry.

As an undercover detective, Kayleen had accumulated a lot of street smarts. She knew what was going on in the drug world and understood the modern perspective on sexuality. I needed information in these areas, and she became my undercover detective.

"Amanda"

My need to understand the public school system led me to Amanda, a schoolteacher. From her I gained knowledge about the fine points of the law. She helped me differentiate between what was acceptable procedure and what was not when I work in schools.

With a quiet, sensitive spirit Amanda had the gift of intercessory prayer, which she exercised on behalf of my ministry. "Let's pray down the gates of hell," she once said.

An unexpected benefit of having Amanda in my core group came from her willingness to help me catch up with correspondence and business details when I got behind. Amanda's prayer was often expressed in deeds of helpfulness.

"Anita"

Even before I decided to enlist individuals as members of a support team, Anita functioned in that capacity. She began to pray for me as soon as I took my ministry on the road.

Many times when I needed encouragement I would sort through the mail to find a note from Anita. A word from her always put a song in my heart even if she said no more than, "I love you, and I'm praying for you."

At church it was not unusual for Anita to greet me with a little package. I'd pretend to object, but really I like surprises.

"I thought of you as soon as I saw this," she would say. I'd open the package and find a book or something that relates to my ministry. That kind of loyalty continued through our relationship as accountability partners.

"Jane"

Teaching a discipleship class together for five years, Jane and I had enjoyed a long-term personal and working relationship. Because of the combination of her profession in nursing and her personality that silently speaks peace, Jane had the ability to calm me down when I experienced a crisis or got riled up from being on the road.

Right after my grandfather's funeral, I had a speaking engagement, and Jane went with me. Along with the grief over my grandfather's sudden death, I was sick.

"I can't do it," I said when I thought about giving my talk.

"Yes, you can," Jane soothed. "First, you're going to eat something and then get some rest." With her help and encouragement I made it through that and other ordeals.

"Shelley"

I chose Shelley because of her people skills and understanding of the corporate world. Shelley holds a high position as a human resource person of a major corporation. When I received an invitation to speak to a group of psychologists and probation officers, I went to Shelley for advice.

"Remember, you will be speaking to professionals, and so you don't need to be quite so dramatic," she said. "Be yourself, but play down the youthful image."

According to Shelley, the corporate world is becoming more aware of the fact that a healthy lifestyle brings greater fulfillment than wealth or prestige. "Present biblical principles without putting in the chapter and verse, and you'll be right on target," she said.

"Karen"

One of my greatest satisfactions in ministry comes from having someone volunteer for service. Therefore I was delighted when Karen said, "I would like to be part of your ministry."

After having breakfast with Karen a couple of times, I learned that indeed her heart was in my area of ministry. Looking ahead to when her own three children would be teens, Karen wanted to prepare herself to help them through the rough times. In the meantime she carried a burden for all the youth of our nation.

As a physician's assistant Karen understood the physical effects of drugs and alcohol. Because of her input, I could speak to students with greater authority on that issue.

Mentors and Role Models

Some of my mentors initiated the relationship. Perhaps God sent Mrs. Jarrett and Marie Strong into my life, but both of them are dead now. If I want someone to act as my coach in ministry, I need to find the right person.

In a mentor I look for someone who does what I do but has progressed farther than I have. The person must also be available and willing to serve in this capacity.

Right now, I don't have anyone in mind to guide me in my ministry with students. When my interest in missions increased, I asked a retired missionary lady if I could call her and ask questions. "I would like that," she said. From her I hope to learn how to increase the effectiveness of my short-term mission trips.

A role model can inspire us to greater achievement without personal interaction. For instance, Dr. James Dobson is one of my role models, although he doesn't even know who I am.

Mother Teresa is somewhere between a mentor and a role model for me. Because she is influential, yet lives simply and keeps her focus on Jesus, my admiration for Mother Teresa grew some years ago to the point I felt compelled to contact her. Not only did I hear from her, but she invited me to bring a group of students to India to work in her homes. A few years later I was privileged to escort another group of mission-minded persons to India, where we interacted with Mother Teresa on three different occasions. What I learned from the brief encounters I had with her continues to shape my ministry.

No matter how much a mentor or role model deserves our adulation, we need to keep our focus on the Lord rather than on human leadership. By depending too much on a mentor or role model we might fall if he or she falls, but we will stand if our hearts are centered on Jesus.

Reader Challenge

• Complete the following diagram with personal information to form a hedge of protection around yourself.

"Form a Hedge of Protection"

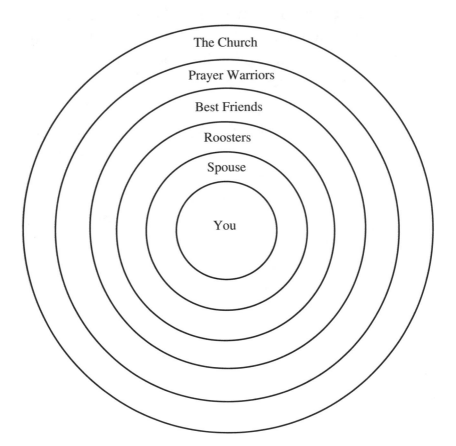

The Church

Prayer Warriors

Best Friends

Roosters

Spouse

You

Form a Hedge of Protection

1. Write your name in the center circle.

2. Write the name of your spouse in one of the outer circles. Chapter 4 will deal with ways you and your spouse can keep each other accountable. For unmarried persons, a close family member or mentor could fill this role.

3. If you have already established accountability partners, write the names of those individuals in the next circle. If you have not yet formed a core group, write names of persons who might help you make wise decisions and preserve your integrity. Will you solicit their involvement in your ministry?

4. Although best friends often lack objectivity, they can augment your ministry with their prayers, love, and support. With your encouragement, they can perhaps point out blind spots you or even your accountability partners do not see. Write their names in the next circle.

5. The names of your prayer warriors go in the next circle. Define how you expect them to contribute to your ministry. Since my assignments require hard work for short periods, I ask everyone to pray when I am on the road. If you face a daily challenge, you might want to enlist one or two persons to pray with you each day of the week or month.

6. The final circle represents the body of Christ or the church. This can be your local church. You might also want to include the name of a role model from the church at large—perhaps someone in your area of ministry who is where you would like to be five years from now.

You will receive your most structured form of accountability through your core group or accountability partners. Here are some of the tools that have helped my group function more efficiently.

• Revise the sample accountability and covenant forms (pages 24 and 26) to meet the needs of your group.

• As you pray the following prayer, concentrate on taking one step toward greater accountability:

DEAR GOD, thank you for Christian friends who will pray for me. Direct me to the person or persons who can make the greatest contribution to my ministry. Help me admit my shortcomings and be willing to take corrective action. Above all, may I keep my heart centered on Jesus as my example. In Jesus' name I pray. Amen.

---

1. Kurt Salierno, *Giving to the Least of These* (Portland, Oregon: Men of Letters, 1991), 92–94.

CHAPTER 3

Personality and Background

After rousing considerable interest on the road with the challenge to find a rooster, I began to wonder: *Who is Kurt Salierno's rooster?* I said to my husband, "Kurt, who is your rooster?"

With his head turned to one side and his hands on his hips, Kurt said, "Lori, do you just sit around thinking up weird questions?"

"No, I'm serious. Remember how the rooster reminded Peter that he had failed his Lord? Who will keep you accountable if you get off track?"

"You."

"Thanks for the compliment, but what if you have a problem with me? Where would you turn?"

"God."

End of conversation. So what did that do to my emphasis on finding accountability partners? I wondered about that passage of scripture that goes something like this: "If I have no influence in my own

house, how can I effectively teach others?" (1 Tim 3:5, Salierno paraphrase).

All I can say is that Kurt Salierno does indeed receive directions from God and has the self-discipline required to carry out his convictions. Because of his personality and background, Kurt is resistant to some of the suggestions I make. Nevertheless, his life demonstrates that God works with different people in different ways. The goal in accountability is to find the most effective method of maintaining a personal relationship with Jesus Christ.

A Hard Lesson

While engaged in street ministry in Portland, Oregon, Kurt began to pray, "Lord, if there is anything in my life that is displeasing to you, please reveal it to me." For several weeks he continued the same prayer without any response from God.[1]

At 2:00 A.M. one morning Kurt had finished presenting the gospel to twelve men who seemed receptive. Encouraged by their interest, he walked down the street eager for another opportunity to share Jesus. A huge, burly man tapped Kurt on the shoulder and said, "Will you talk to me?"

No one could have done anything to please Kurt more. Most of the time Kurt had to search for listeners. This man took the initiative. "Yes, let's talk," Kurt said excitedly.

"Good. Come to my room, and let's talk."

The tone of the man's voice when he said "talk"

sent a shiver down Kurt's spine. Dark memories of a homosexual who had tried to involve Kurt during his youth bombarded his mind. Suddenly, all the anger and hatred built up from his earlier encounter exploded. Kurt looked the man in the eyes and spit at him: "I hate you! No, I will not go to your room and talk!"

As Kurt walked away, conflicting emotions churned within his heart. How could he feel so much love one moment and so much hatred the next?

A tap on the shoulder intensified his emotions. "Will you talk to me?" the man persisted.

Without answering, Kurt continued to walk and pray. "God, the week has gone so well. Why did you put me into a situation like this?"

As soon as Kurt uttered the prayer, a light came on in his mind. Had he not asked for divine revelation of anything in his life that was displeasing to God? Suddenly, he knew he needed to get rid of his hatred for homosexuals. But how?

Tapping Kurt on the shoulder for the third time, the stranger urged, "Talk to me! Won't you talk to me?"

"God, if this is an open door, direct me through it. Fill me with the kind of compassion and love you have for this man," Kurt prayed.

As soon as Kurt felt God's leading, he suggested they talk on the street. The man would have no part of it. Finally, Kurt placed his life in God's hands. "Okay, we'll go to your room and talk."

Allowing the man to lead him to a building four blocks away, Kurt felt a mixture of fear and hatred tinged with compassion. An intense drama was about to begin. As the leading man, Kurt depended solely on his Director.

"Come to bed and let's talk," the man ordered after securely locking the door.

"I'm here to talk, to talk about Jesus," Kurt declared, and then he proceeded to preach a powerful sermon under the anointing of the Holy Spirit. He quoted verses from the Bible and spoke of God's love. "I want to show you how much Jesus loves you."

For all the response he received, Kurt might as well have been talking to a statue. Trying to break the silence, Kurt said, "Okay, you heard me. What do you have to say for yourself?"

Much to Kurt's surprise, tears began to roll down the stranger's face. Words finally tumbled out to reveal a past filled with perversions of every kind. "I wanted to rape you. I was going to kill you." His voice softened. "Then you talked to me about Jesus and how he loves me."

Kurt tried to tell him that God would forgive him and he could start a new life, but the man said, "No, I've done too many bad things."

All persuasive effort failed. Finally, the man extended his hand. "Kurt, thanks for coming up and ... talking to me." With that he unlocked the door, opened it, and said, "Go on, get out."

Outside the room, Kurt rejoiced in his freedom. Through a hard lesson, God had revealed a hindering factor in Kurt's ministry and helped him overcome his hatred for homosexuals.

Besides receiving signals directly from God, Kurt has for many years had accountability in a general sense rather than the more specific form of accountability I advocate. While an associate pastor, Kurt was accountable to the senior pastor as well as to the governing boards of the church. Now that he is a senior pastor, he is even more accountable to the governing board of the church.

In analyzing my husband's experience I concluded that his approach to accountability was different than mine, but effective. Still, I wanted to see him more deeply involved in accountability strategies.

About a year after Kurt and I had the conversation in which he resisted the more structured form of accountability, my husband began to take steps in that direction. First, he attended a conference sponsored by Promise Keepers, a national men's ministry. Observing the value that others receive from support groups, Kurt went one step further. The man who wanted to answer only to God or me has begun to dialogue with another man regarding the tough issues that confront today's pastors.

Praise the Lord! If Kurt Salierno can be persuaded to seek divine guidance through human interaction, I believe anyone can benefit from a structured system of accountability.

The Macho Image

From a cultural standpoint, men have long been taught they must be tough. When little girls cried, they were comforted, but tears were discouraged in little boys. "Big boys don't cry," they have been told. While the general philosophy is now changing, traditions die hard. Many men still feel the need to maintain a macho image.

For once, society and the church are on the same side. Men need to open up and express their emotions. They need to reveal their hurts and disappointments and receive encouragement and inspiration from each other.

The popularity of Promise Keepers, started by football coach Bill McCartney,[2] is helping men break free from the stoic stereotype of pretense. The sports hero who promotes integrity, marital fidelity, and spiritual leadership in the home is no sissy. If he can admit the need for moral support, other men are more willing to take off their plastic smiles and deal with the garbage accumulated in their past.

When a discussion of Promise Keepers came up in my core group, Shelley said, "My husband has been leading a group like that for four years. Not only has it been good for him, it has been good for me as well."

Shelley explained that the accountability group takes the place of a nagging wife and is far more effective. "I don't have to play God and try to mold my husband's spiritual life," she said. Through an exchange of information, the men discover what changes they need to make in their lives. "If you think the accountability sheet we fill out calls for specifics, you should see what the men use," Shelley said to the group.

Recognizing the influence that entertainment has on human behavior, the men discuss what movies and television they have watched. Watching an R-rated movie will cause someone to ask, "Why did you need to watch that?" Through a series of questions and honest answers, the man begins to understand the need to replace that kind of entertainment with edifying activities.

While some of the men in the group are introverts, the outgoing personality of the leader encourages them to open up. In a non-threatening environment where everyone is confirmed rather than condemned, it becomes easier to share their pain and even cry together. As they reveal their brokenness, they help each other claim victory through Christ.

The aspect of the program that brought the greatest response from the other women was the emphasis on husband-wife relationships. Some of the questions promised personal dividends: Did you hug your wife today? Were you kind and considerate of your wife? How are you doing in the romance department?

Those questions might conjure up thoughts of roses and jewels, but Kurt's support of me is of far more value than the rarest diamond. Again, Kurt often comes through in top-notch form on his own initiative.

As one of my college seminars got underway, good things began to happen. I called Kurt. "Classes have been cancelled for two days so the students can focus on their spiritual needs," I said, projecting the enthusiasm I felt inside.

"Maybe you'll need to stay a couple of weeks and let God really bring revival," Kurt said. That might have sounded as though my husband wanted to get rid of me, but he quickly added, "I couldn't get along without you that long. If you stay, I'll fly out to be with you." Nothing transpired from Kurt's suggestion, but he proved his loyalty by his willingness to sacrifice.

Of course, it is equally important for women to ask similar questions. Am I being a good wife? How can I show greater support for my husband? If a husband and wife are both involved in accountability groups, the prospect for improved relations doubles.

Whether a group is composed of men or women, members learn from each other. Inhibitions diminish as mutual sharing occurs. If necessary, they confront each other to bring wayward ones back to the fold. New Christians learn stability from seasoned saints who, in turn, pick up enthusiasm from those new in the faith.

A Private Person

The male gender is not entirely to blame for reluctance to become involved in an accountability group. Many women balk at what they consider to be an invasion of privacy. "Unless God personally sent me a telegram, I just wouldn't do it," said a woman I'll call Juliann (not her real name).

Because of her strong Christian commitment, Juliann provides an interesting study into how personality relates to accountability. Even though information is difficult to obtain from such a private person, her lifestyle and her limited comments offer suggestions about staying strong spiritually so that we might benefit others in similar circumstances.

People who have known her most of her life report that Juliann was the ideal child—always obedient, never in any trouble. She accepted Jesus as her Savior at an early age and willingly followed the teachings of Christian parents. The program of discipline established during childhood carried over into adulthood.

Extremely gifted in music, Juliann dedicated her talents to the Lord at a young age. Ministering through her music continues to be a joy rather than a burden. "My lowest times come when I don't have an opportunity to serve," she said.

Juliann's home-based business shields her from the ungodly influence of the world. "It's easier to keep my mind on the Lord in the home environment," she said. "When I turn on the television, I usually listen to a Christian station. That helps me keep tuned in with God."

From her earliest remembrance, prayer has been important to Juliann. Communication with God became even more vital during several crises involving life and death situations. "Many times I couldn't have made it without the Lord and Christian friends who prayed with me and my family," she said.

When it comes to prayers, Juliann will take all she can get. Although speaking out in a group intimidates her, she never hesitates to share a prayer request with her Bible study class. When faced with surgery, she asked to be anointed for healing. At the same time she did not even reveal the problem to her best friend.

So—how does this disciplined woman of faith struggle? "My biggest struggle right now is trying to compete with the world to raise godly children." With two kids in college, Juliann is uncomfortable giving them the freedom required to function. A tendency to be over-protective sometimes gets in the way of a harmonious parent-child relationship. "If I had my way, I'd know where my kids are every minute, but I can't do that. It's hard, but I'm learning to trust God for their physical and spiritual safety every time they leave the house," she said.

Resolution of one problem area proves that Juliann's system of accountability works. "My sensitive nature used to cause me a lot of unnecessary grief," she said. "I would cry for hours over a remark that I likely misunderstood in the first place." Keeping her focus on God has freed her from the need to strive for human approval.

I include Juliann's story in this chapter in recognition of those whose personality types are a barrier to participation in the form of accountability I recommend. At the same time I would point out that reserved individuals in my discipleship classes have been delightfully surprised at the benefit they received when they made an effort to open up to others.

Some people are actually engaged in accountability without realizing it. Even talking with a strong Christian when they are discouraged or leaning on a friend during a crisis is casually structured accountability. Although I don't want to take a legalistic approach, I would urge reticent individuals to move one step beyond where they are in the area of accountability.

Blended Personalities

My core group in Phoenix represented a variety of personality types ranging from extrovert to introvert, with most of the members somewhere in between. Amanda described herself as an introvert. As a teacher, Amanda functioned well on a professional level. In ministry, she took an up-front role as an accomplished pianist or gifted soloist. On a personal level, however, fear held her back from revealing her inner self.

Before joining my group, Amanda had one close friend in whom she confided. "When I was down, she could usually pull me out," Amanda said. "Except, if I was really going through a crisis, I tended to withdraw even from her. As a result, I faced life alone when I needed help the most."

A few months before I formed my group, Amanda had had an experience so dramatic it could have been directed only by the Lord. As events began to unfold,

Amanda was forced to move beyond her comfort zone. It seemed that God pushed her forward one step at a time, compelling Amanda to make the next move. At one point the action required was too radical even to consider without prayer support. On her own initiative, Amanda put together a prayer team—a considerable feat in itself for one who avoided reaching out to others for help.

While making plans for our first retreat, I approached Amanda. "Would you like to tell the story you told me to our entire group?" I asked.

"Lori, you know how scared I get."

"Yes, I know, but forget about yourself. Tell the story from God's point of view."

Although quite nervous, Amanda gave a compelling testimony at the retreat. She has also consented to share her story in another chapter of this book. The support she received from the other women convinced Amanda of the value of interacting with others on an intimate level.

Through her involvement with the group, Amanda also overcame her fear of praying in public. Just prior to a Christmas Eve service, my grandfather had been rushed to the hospital at the point of death. As I tried to lead the corporate prayer, I was overcome by emotion. Kurt came forward and took over.

During that time Amanda went through a personal struggle. One second too late she made her decision to act. "If Kurt hadn't come to your rescue, I would have stepped forward to lead the prayer," she told me later.

Observing Amanda's progress from reluctance to pray with six people to willingness to pray in front of hundreds was gratifying indeed. Amanda proved that someone with a reserved personality can adapt to an accountability group and become more outgoing in the process.

Reader Challenge

• On a scale of 1 to 10 (with 10 representing the extrovert), rate your personality. How does your personality affect your willingness to get involved in an accountability group?

• If you reject group involvement at this time, will you ask God to show you how you can receive a surge of fresh spiritual vitality? Will you ask God what changes you need to make and then remain open to divine direction? Will you cultivate the self-discipline necessary to carry out Gods directives?

• Be creative in developing a spiritual relationship with others. After I spoke to a group of high school students in Florida, I received a letter from Kristi Hardee. "I am doing my hour of power. It is really neat," she wrote. This young woman who takes Christianity seriously gets up at five o'clock each morning and calls two of her friends, who each call two other friends. The seven people pray at the same time for an hour each day. Kristi reports that this practice is "making an impact on our lives."

• Would you become involved in an accountability group if the right person gave you a nudge? If so, will you pray for God to direct such a person to you?

• Men only: Does your masculinity get in the way of joining an accountability group? Are you willing to relinquish control of your life to God? Will you allow others to help you nurture your relationship with the Lord?

• Has your background programmed your mind with Christian values? If not, you will need to take extreme care to counteract the world's influence on your life. How will you do this?

• Write out one step you will take to promote your own spiritual growth. The sermon or lesson you are preparing to present to others may provide a clue.

• Revise the following prayer to your needs:

HEAVENLY FATHER, thank you for my personality that makes me unique. Help me to maximize the strengths of my personality type and minimize the weaknesses. If I need someone in my life to bring me to greater accountability, direct that person to me. Help me to be receptive to divine instruction whether it comes directly from the Holy Spirit or through a human channel. Help me discover the most effective means of keeping a fresh relationship with you. In Jesus' name I pray. Amen.

1. Salierno, 83–88.
2. Bill McCartney and Dave Diles, *From Ashes to Glory* (Nashville:Thomas Nelson, Inc.), 1995.

CHAPTER 4

Spousal Spiritual Thermometers

In a small-group Bible study the leader asked, "What were some of the hardships the Apostle Paul had to endure that might have caused him to become discouraged?"

A few members had responded with typical answers when one lady said, "Paul wasn't blessed with a wife."

Laughter followed along with a few light-hearted comments, but the lady had made the remark in all seriousness. She had a point. Who is in a better position to check vital signs than a spouse?

According to 1 Corinthians 7:14, "the unbelieving husband is made holy through his wife, and the unbelieving wife is made holy through her husband." Since a Christian can lead an unbeliever to the Lord, surely two Christians can contribute to the spiritual well-being of each other. With an intentional effort by both husband and wife, the possibility will become a reality.

When my husband, Kurt, tries to take my spiritual temperature, I sometimes want to grab the thermometer and smash it to pieces. Still, I have to admit that Kurt looks out only for my best interests—both physically and spiritually.

One time Kurt and I were at a party. As often happens, the men had gathered on one side of the room and the women on the other. Each group engaged in conversation that appealed to the particular gender. In our group, the personal affairs of one of the ladies in the church came up.

Several of the women had already commented when I said, "Let me tell you the latest. I talked to her yesterday and...." I could feel my husband's eyes on me. Why wasn't he talking with the men or at least listening, I wondered.

Now, Kurt could have been enough of a diplomat to dash to my side, throw an arm around my shoulder and say, "Sweetheart, let's integrate this party." That isn't Kurt's style. Across the room he pointed his finger directly at me and said in a stern tone of voice, "Lori, that's enough!"

With my mouth half open and my arms outstretched in gesture, I froze as though paralyzed.

"Tell us, tell us!" someone prompted.

"I can't," I said in a small voice I couldn't even recognize as my own.

As soon as we got in the car my emotions exploded. "Kurt Salierno!" I sputtered, "how dare you embarrass me in front of my friends?" Neither defending himself nor condemning me, Kurt allowed me to vent my frustration. When I ran out of words, I threatened, "I'm taking this to my prayer time."

"Good," Kurt said. "Let me know what God says."

When I tried to tell the Lord how unfair my husband had been, God bounced the words right back at me. Not until I acknowledged my guilt of nearly betraying a confidence and asked God to forgive me for that did peace descend on my soul. For the time being, though, I decided to keep the result of my prayer effort just between God and me.

"So—how did you make out with God regarding our little discussion?" Kurt finally asked.

I shrugged my shoulders in surrender. "God agreed with you," I confessed.

Kurt smiled and folded me into his arms. All trace of the rift between us dissolved, and I felt God's approval surround me. Let me explain some of the lessons I learned from this experience.

Private Retreat

Though it was hard for me to accept at the time, Kurt helped me avoid blabbing plain old gossip. If I had talked out of turn at that moment, many people would, sooner or later, wonder whether they could tell me anything in confidence.

I only partially regret exploding at him on the way home. I think he knows now that the diplomacy he did not show on that occasion could be interpreted as lack of respect. Couples who effectively practice mutual accountability do so with high regard for each other and not as stern taskmasters. By no means is Kurt my taskmaster, stern or otherwise, but we are both growing in what it means to be mutually accountable for our words and our actions.

During one of my seminars in a church out of town I spoke with the youth pastor and his wife about the need for leaders to be more accountable for the lifestyle they project to the world. We discussed the importance of accountability in marriage. As indicated by my own experience, a spouse can point out a fault or shortcoming that calls for correction. In addition, compromise and mutual support provide the direction needed to maintain accountability as a team.

The youth pastor and his wife had already developed a personal program to keep them in tune with each other and with the Lord. With their permission I pass along some of the ideas shared by Mark and Vickie Shaner.[1]

Every two to three years the Shaners put their busy careers on hold, arrange care for their two children, and steal away for a three-day retreat. In a quiet atmosphere with no telephone or television, they concentrate solely on each other and God. To help them keep their focus they even restrict eating to a mere sustenance level.

When asked what led to their decision to conduct a private marriage retreat, Mark responded. "We had been married about two years and had just graduated from college when we began work as youth ministers. Sometimes our ideas conflicted about how youth ministry should be done."

"We're talking major conflict," Vickie interrupted.

"Yeah—like the kind that ends up in a divorce court," Mark said.

In detecting a problem early, Mark and Vickie had taken the first step toward resolution. Too often church leaders pretend all is well until the marriage falls apart and sends a message to the world that Christians are no different from non-Christians.

At a youth workers' convention the Shaners captured a vision that changed their lives. One of the speakers stressed the importance of striking a balance between marriage and ministry. According to the speaker, stability could be achieved through periods of intense communication between husband, wife, and God.

Mark and Vickie break discussion time into four segments, each two hours long. During each session they focus on one particular issue. That leaves plenty of time for reading, relaxation, and romance. They return home as lovers and have a better understanding of themselves as persons, partners, parents, and professionals.

Persons and Partners

After making the necessary arrangements, the Shaners drive to their selected hideaway on a

Thursday morning, which fits their schedule. On the way they discuss any unfinished business on the home front. With details of routine living out of the way, they can then concentrate on the agenda designed to put new life into their marriage.

On Thursday afternoon they direct their attention to how they are doing as persons and partners. "Am I too involved in my career to meet your need?" they ask each other.

"In marriage it's easy to live separate lives," Mark said. "We live in the same house and share the same check book, but we live in two separate worlds where our paths seldom cross."

That comment hit home because it certainly applied to my own situation. Not only are Kurt and I involved in separate areas of ministry, my work takes me away from home far too much of the time. Some people question the wisdom of what I do. Sometimes I wonder myself what I'm doing on the road instead of spending the time with Kurt.

When I am lonely, my solace comes from knowing my work is sanctioned by both God and my husband. If Kurt objected to my travels, I would discontinue holding seminars because I know God would not want me to jeopardize my marriage. In agreement with each other and with God, Kurt and I decided I could be most effective presenting the gospel during short-term assignments wherever I'm called. We're both willing to make the required sacrifices to reach lost souls for Jesus Christ.

To compensate for the time we must spend apart, Kurt and I devote an extra portion of quality time to each other after I return from a trip. Such an arrangement isn't for everyone, but it works for us.

In fact, Kurt once observed that we actually spend more time together than many couples who are never separated because we intentionally make time for each other. Except for the few occasions I am on extended travel, Kurt and I reserve three slots each week as our time to be together.

Since Monday is Kurt's day off, we try to do something to create a lasting memory. It may be as simple as working on a project together, exploring virgin territory, or sharing a picnic lunch in an unusual setting. I look back on many of those events and think of them as our "Memories on Monday."

Of all our activities our "date" night excites me most. I agree with the couple who hung a plaque in their dining room that read, in essence: "Marriage is falling in love over and over again, but always with the same person." Kurt and I usually begin our date by going out to dinner. We might take in a movie if we can find one that doesn't compromise our standards. Whatever we do, we concentrate on having fun and finding ways to inject new life into our romance.

Our third weekly contact is more like a business meeting where we go over our calendars. Kurt keeps me informed of his schedule, and I ask him what he thinks about dates for speaking engagements that

have come up for me. Together we make plans to keep us headed in the right direction and avoid conflicts in our schedules. When Kurt and I focus on each other as persons, we sometimes need to address our differences. I think God shows a terrific sense of humor in bringing opposite personality types together. Reaching an agreement can become a challenge.

Not long after Kurt and I married, one of our differences surfaced. Kurt's idea of being on time is to arrive fifteen minutes early. I don't like to waste time, so I try to arrive at church or an appointment at the specified moment. That usually means I'm five minutes late, but that's close enough for me.

One Sunday morning Kurt and I argued all the way to church. "Why can't you be on time just once?" Kurt said.

"I am on time. Nothing ever happens the first few minutes anyway."

"That's because of people like you!" Kurt retorted.

Our emotions showed on our faces as we walked into church. One of the men questioned my husband about the problem.

"I had to wait twenty minutes for that woman (me)," Kurt fumed.

That sensitive, brilliant man suggested the perfect solution. "Get yourself another car," he whispered. "It'll put harmony into your marriage."

Kurt bought a second car and ordered a special license plate that read HARMONY. Bless his heart!

Not all conflicts can be resolved so easily. With creativity, compromise, understanding, and guidance from the Holy Spirit, though, it's possible to reach a consensus that leaves room for both persons to express their individuality.

Parents

On Friday morning Mark and Vickie turn their attention to parenting. "How do we relate with each of the children on a personal level and as a team?" they ask themselves. "Are the children making the most of their strong points?" "Are we doing all we can to help them progress in weak areas?" For two hours the Shaners focus on the best way to nurture their children on physical, emotional, intellectual, and spiritual levels. Since Kurt and I don't have children, I transferred the theme of this session to family problems in general.

We had been married about five years when I received a call advising me of a family crisis that played havoc with my emotions. Not only did I disagree with how the problem had been evaluated, I objected to how it was being handled. I voiced my opinion over the phone and vowed to distance myself from the situation.

As I poured out my resentment and frustration to Kurt, he interrupted. "You need to go home right away. Your family needs your support."

I made several excuses that Kurt vetoed with sound reasoning. Finally, I said, "We don't have the money." He certainly couldn't argue with that.

So—what did my ingenious husband do? He sold his boat and bought me a plane ticket from Indiana to Vancouver, Washington. For Kurt Salierno, that represented the ultimate sacrifice. To him, fishing practically equates with survival. When I was unable to make an objective judgment, Kurt made it for me. That kind of commitment to the welfare of the family keeps a marriage on track.

Professionals

After a simple lunch, requiring little preparation, and a period of recreation, Mark and Vickie sit down on Friday afternoon to look at themselves as professionals. "Does your career provide you with emotional and spiritual fulfillment?" they ask each other. "What disappointments do you face?" "How can I help?"

Just prior to one retreat Mark had taken part of the youth group on a short-term mission trip. "Mark told me how the girls conducted themselves," Vickie said. "Modesty is out and immorality is in. Youth pastors are vulnerable in this area. I asked Mark, 'What is my role in helping you resist temptation?' "

Mark cast his wife an admiring glance. "Vic does very well in handling her role," he said.

Indeed, each partner can reduce temptation for his or her spouse by preserving physical and emotional appeal. When an attractive mate waits at home, the charm of someone offering adventure begins to fade. The husband or wife who expresses love in ever new and exciting ways encourages a spouse to keep romantic interest at home.

Sometimes the focus on careers requires one or both persons to make a decision of lasting importance. In order to renew her teaching certificate, Vickie needed to take some classes, but it was difficult to go back to school with two small children. "If it hadn't been for the marriage retreat, I probably would have let my teaching certificate slide," Vickie said. "Since we jointly decided it was important, Mark was part of helping me bring the goal to reality."

I could certainly relate with Vickie's experience. If it hadn't been for Kurt's initiative, my hopes of earning a master's degree would probably have fizzled out. We were in Indiana when I began to investigate where I might complete my education. After checking out several graduate schools, I told Kurt my preference leaned toward one on the west coast. That was a long way from Indiana, and my faith didn't quite go that far.

The distance detail didn't phase Kurt. "We'll just pray that God will open the door for you to go there," he said.

While we were praying, we received an invitation to go to Phoenix—closer to the west coast, but still not there. At first Kurt declined the offer, but then he thought of a plan. "Would you be willing to fly between Phoenix and the west coast?"

I didn't like the idea of being separated from Kurt during the week, but there were some positive factors to consider. My grandparents lived in the area; so I wouldn't have a housing problem. I could fly out

Monday morning, stay with my grandparents through Thursday, and fly back to Phoenix Friday evening. Also, my brother attended the same school and could help me deal with Kurt's absence.

Still, I was reluctant to make that kind of commitment, but Kurt was adamant. "Lori, you may not have a choice because we are *going* to get your education. If this is the opportunity God is providing, we can't afford to pass it by." Convinced by his reasoning, I agreed we should move to Phoenix. Subsequently, I enrolled in graduate school on the west coast.

For the next two years I lived on an emotional roller coaster. Every time I felt like quitting (which was often), I remembered Kurt was counting on me. I could not allow him to waste his emotional and financial investment in me. Regardless of the cost, I had to keep going until the day came when we both rejoiced. My diploma should show Kurt's name beside mine.

Priorities

During the final Saturday morning segment of the retreat, the Shaners ask themselves, "Where are we going from here?" "What are our priorities?"

As they do in each session, Vickie and Mark pull out the notebook where they have recorded past priorities. They praise the Lord for progress made. If they failed to meet a goal, they ask, "Was it too hard to meet?" "Did it represent reality or merely a dream?" "Should we work on it again or chuck the whole idea?"

A few years after Kurt placed priority on my education to further my career, I had an opportunity to return the favor, but I failed to respond as quickly.

When Kurt first mentioned his desire to move from serving as a youth pastor to leading as a senior pastor, I discouraged him. "You don't want to do that," I said. "You love the youth, and you're doing a great work." That was true, of course, but my motive was geared more toward my interest rather than toward what was best for my husband. I did not want to leave Phoenix. Neither did I want to assume the role of a senior pastor's wife.

At first Kurt didn't push the issue, but the topic kept coming up on our date nights. Comments such as, "Lori, if I were a senior pastor, I would do this or that," told me his dream still lived.

I tried to ignore the message I was hearing, but eventually I had to ask myself, *Am I being supportive in trying to channel Kurt's ambition in a different direction?* Finally, I got tired of the nagging guilt and decided to open up the subject for discussion. "Kurt," I said, "when I think of you as a senior pastor, I get uncomfortable. That's not my choice because I like being in Phoenix, but—"

Kurt didn't wait for me to finish. "Lori, I'm feeling a need to do something different."

"I sensed that, and I want you to know I'll support you in your decision. You supported me, and now it's my turn to support you."

After Kurt and I prayed, a sense of peace settled over me. While I wasn't overwhelmed with joy, I no longer dreaded to make a move. I knew God would direct us to the place that would be right for Kurt. Besides, the move would not hinder my career because I could operate from any place with a nearby major airport. At that point I put Kurt's career first just as he had put my education first.

To keep on track spiritually and in harmony with each other, a couple needs to make an intentional effort to maintain open communication lines. There are different ways to accomplish this goal. Kurt and I stay on course through our three weekly events while the Shaners periodically retreat for a longer period of intense dialogue. Of course, Mark and Vickie work out routine problems as they occur, just as Kurt and I sometimes extend our time of togetherness.

If you and your spouse write notes on your own marriage retreat, your notebook will become a tool to extend the value of your retreat until the next time you steal away to be alone. "Because we have everything on file, the retreat isn't over on Saturday night," Vickie said.

"We don't pull out the notebook every day and beat each other over the head with it," Mark added, "but we do review our progress from time to time." As they record their goals on paper, they hide them in their hearts as well, and God becomes part of bringing the goals to pass.

An Organized Program

The Marriage Encounter or Marriage Seminar offers an alternative approach to developing a communication system that acts as a spiritual thermometer. In a setting with other couples, someone leads the agenda and asks questions designed to bring two people to a better understanding of each other. When the temperature registers below normal, corrective action will bring it up to the healthy zone.

After we were married about ten years, Kurt and I attended a Marriage Seminar. We went because it was part of the program of the church we attended at the time, but it was a positive experience for both of us. My most vivid memory is Kurt's answer to the question: "What do you look forward to in your marriage?" Kurt wrote, " I look forward to growing old with you because you will never be boring. Even when we're in rocking chairs, you will still be full of surprises."

I see the Marriage Encounter or Marriage Seminar as a good place to start for those who feel over-whelmed by the thought of launching out on their own. After a formal experience, possibly a private retreat will seem less formidable.

A comment made by a pastor's wife in the divorce court stresses the importance of finding a balance between ministry and marriage. Speaking to her husband, the tearful wife said, "You had so many books on your shelf about ministry, but you had no books on your shelf about marriage."

Could a point be made more emphatic than that?

Reader Challenge

• If you are married and have been reading this chapter alone, perhaps you would like to re-read it with your spouse. As you read together, think in terms of your own marriage relationship.

• When you finish, pray together for direction and then answer the following questions:

√ Can we set aside specific times on a weekly basis to build our relationship?

√ What times would work for our schedule?

√ Would a retreat work better in our situation? (Especially if you have children, the distractions of home life may make it difficult to devote time to each other on an appointment schedule.)

√ When can we go on a retreat? (Try to make it soon.)

√ Where can we go to find privacy? (It need not be an expensive place. The Shaners have gone to state parks, a cabin loaned by a friend, or to a motel in the off-season. They suggest a distance away from home that will require a one-to two-hour drive. "Otherwise our minds would drift back to work," Mark said.)

√ What preparations should we make? (Find someone to baby-sit the children. Take simple foods such as fruit, cheese, and crackers to reduce preparation and cleanup time. Light meals result in a partial fast, which will remind you to focus on God and each other. Take along books, games, bikes— whatever you need for recreation.)

√ How shall we structure our time together? (Use the guidelines provided by Mark and Vickie and adapt the questions to your particular situation. Buy a notebook and divide it into four sections. Label a section for each of the four sessions. During each discussion period keep notes of the conversation. The following summary of the Shaners guidelines will help you tailor the questions to your needs.)

Guidelines for Accountability in Marriage
by Mark and Vickie Shaner

Persons and Partners

Am I too involved in my career to meet your need? How can we find common ground to bridge our differences?

Parents

How do we relate with each of the children on a personal level and as a team? Are the children making the most of their strong points? Are we doing all we can to help them progress in weak areas?

Professionals

Does your career provide you with emotional and spiritual fulfillment? What disappointments do you face? How can I help?

Priorities

Where are we going from here? What are our priorities? Where do we want to be in a year? Five years? Ten?

• As you focus on your marriage as a device to keep you accountable to God, will you pray this prayer?

GOD, we thank you for bringing us together as husband and wife, and for the privilege of serving you as a team. Show us how to help each other be more effective in ministry. If one of us stumbles, guide the other one in lifting up the fallen one. In Jesus' name we pray. Amen.

1. The Shaners are available for consultation and can be reached at 1590 27th Ave.; Vero Beach, FL 32960.

CHAPTER 5

Sensuality in the Sanctuary

Although it is true, a statement once made in *Focus on the Family Magazine* came across as a startling concept. "Sex begins in church," the author wrote.

After our initial surprise subsides, we recognize that indeed church is the best place for sex to begin. What better place than in the sanctuary to discover God's wonderful gift of sexuality?

Two people who learn to love the Lord early in life are in an ideal position to taste of romantic love. Perhaps they meet in a Bible study group where they concentrate on practical application of biblical principles. An attraction develops, and they begin to date. In due time they pledge their love to each other for a lifetime. Although they desire each other sexually, they avoid situations that would generate temptation. By waiting until marriage they experience sex as God intended it to be.

It's a beautiful picture. Unfortunately, Satan also invades the sanctuary with his version of sexuality.

Satan uses a more subtle approach in church than he does in the world, where he promotes immorality and perversion as normal behavior. For instance, a woman comes to the pastor for counseling. As she pours out a tale of sorrow, emotion overwhelms her, and tears begin to flow. The tears arouse the pastor's sympathy. Placing an arm around the distraught woman's shoulders, he comforts her with understanding words.

That is how a minister's downfall often begins. The bond that develops from sharing in a crisis strengthens until one or both persons entertain romantic notions. If not curtailed, physical desire can lead to sin.

Precautionary Measures

According to an old legend, a king spread word throughout the kingdom that he wanted to hire a chauffeur for his wife and children. Applicants lined up at the palace.

During each interview the king asked the same question. Suppose you are driving up a steep mountain. When you reach the top, you discover an unprotected drop-off at the edge of the road. How close to the edge can you safely drive?

"Twelve inches," one man said. Other applicants boasted they could come as close as three inches from the edge without plunging the passengers to death.

When he heard such answers, the king abruptly ended the interview. Finally, one man said, "Your Majesty, I don't know how close to the edge I could come. I always keep as far away from danger as I can."

"Ah," said the king, "you are the one I have been looking for." Then he called to his servant, "Bring my wife and children to meet their chauffeur."

By avoiding the danger zone Christian leaders can guard against falling into a trap. It is up to each individual to develop a set of guidelines that will work in his or her situation.

One man established certain rules to apply any time he met with a woman. Although his door was closed, he instructed his secretary to enter the office every ten or fifteen minutes during a session. She did not interrupt except to make her presence felt while she selected a book from the library or placed a letter in the file.

"I always kept the desk between me and the woman," he said. "No matter what happened I did not violate that rule. If a woman burst into tears, I would call in my secretary and say, 'So-and-so needs a hug.' My secretary would then take over."

A pastor in a small church without a secretary left the door open when counseling with women. The open door signified a more professional, less intimate environment.

After serving with her husband for nearly fifty years in the pastoral ministry, a widow said, "I never

counseled with a man alone, and I don't believe my husband ever counseled with a woman alone." Their policy left no room for impropriety to develop and prevented rumors from getting started. Frankly, these days call for leaving the door ajar no matter which gender is being counseled.

Precautionary measures are necessary even if we do not feel we are susceptible to temptation. Married to Kurt Salierno, I cannot imagine ever being attracted to another man. Get involved? Me? Never! No way! Yet I read, "If you think you are standing, watch out that you do not fall" (1 Cor 10:12). My relationship with Kurt is too precious to allow any room for error.

Misplaced Trust

In suggesting the need for caution I almost feel like an alcoholic promoting temperance. With my trusting nature how can I expect anyone who knows how I operate to take me seriously when I say, "Be careful?"

I grew up believing everyone who came to church truly wanted to worship the Lord. It has been difficult for me to learn that some people have a different agenda.

Particularly in matters of sexuality, my eyes have been opened. When I relate with men, I don't think in terms of extramarital affairs or perversion. I want to be able to demonstrate the love of God to everyone without being misunderstood. Too often I have found that to be impossible.

One time I came back from a trip on the road still incensed by an encounter with a certain man. To my core group I said, "How dare anyone treat me that way!"

I continued to express my indignation until Kayleen interrupted. "Oh, Lori, cut it!"

Her reaction surprised me. "What are you talking about?"

"Get real. You are so naive. Sometimes your friendliness comes across as flirtatious. When you think you're building a bridge to the gospel, men are building a bridge to the bed." Before I could absorb the impact of that statement, Kayleen continued to educate me about the motives of men.

Stunned by what I was hearing, I started to cry. "I can't believe men think that way."

"They do, and it's high time you expect certain reactions. If you don't like it, then make the change from your end." In loving terms, Kayleen described the way I needed to start thinking. "Be wary of friendly gestures from a man," she said. "Ask the Holy Spirit to show you the line where safety ends and danger begins. As soon as anyone crosses that line, back off immediately."

How could someone who wasn't "churchy" offer such sound spiritual advice? I wondered. Would I ever learn to understand the worldly view of sexuality as well as Kayleen had learned to apply spiritual truths to life? The challenge still makes me feel uncomfortable at times.

Hard Lessons

Concepts completely foreign to my nature are difficult for me to grasp in one lesson. Life, however, continues to provide me with opportunities to advance my education.

An incident that happened in a church I called home at the time helped reinforce what I had already been taught. After I finished speaking one Sunday morning, a man came up to me and said, "You almost persuaded me to become a Christian today."

Nothing thrills my heart more than leading someone to Jesus Christ—especially someone who has been resistant to the gospel. Perhaps my prayers, combined with those of his wife and family, were about to be answered. Together we could surely overcome whatever obstacle stood in his way. "What kept you from making a commit-ment to Christ?" I asked.

"I can't decide if it's the Holy Spirit or emotion working on me," he said.

I had a ready answer for that. "The Holy Spirit uses emotion," I said. "When you fell in love with your wife, that was emotion that brought you to a deeper commitment. In the same way you can come to Jesus Christ."

As I continued to explain how emotion can lead us to the Lord, the man suddenly interrupted.

"There's only one problem. I listen to you, and I'm drawn to Jesus, but there's a conflict going on."

"What's that?"

I wish I could revise his answer, but there doesn't seem to be a way to refine such crude language. Looking straight into my eyes, he said, "I lust after your body."

His words took me totally off guard, but I averted his eyes and tried to ignore the remark. "Let's talk about what's keeping you from Christ," I said.

Not willing to change the subject, the man wanted to know how to handle his desire, which he expressed in even more explicit terms. At that point my evangelistic zeal waned, and my self-preservation instinct took over. Out of the corner of my eye I could see my husband, Kurt, driving up in his Jeep. Surely, my Prince Charming would rescue me.

"Lori, are you ready to go to lunch?" Kurt asked.

"Yes. In fact, I'm ready to go right now."

The two men exchanged greetings. "Your wife almost persuaded me to become a Christian today, and right now I'm talking to her about that commitment," the man said to Kurt.

"Good," Kurt said. Turning to me, he said, "When you're finished, meet me at the restaurant." Then he drove off. So much for Prince Charming.

Desperate to escape from the situation, I noticed the man's wife nearby and moved to join her. As soon as I could graciously end the three-way conversation, I suggested that the man contact a certain man in the

congregation if he had further questions about making a commitment to Christ.

My emotions churned as I drove to meet Kurt. Why must sensuality complicate presentation of the gospel?

When I tried to tell Kurt what happened, I cleaned up the language so much that he did not comprehend what took place. Not wanting to jeopardize Kurt's relationship with the man, I took the matter to my group of women.

The discussion that followed helped me gain a better perspective on the issue. While I cannot control another's thoughts, I can discourage them by the way I dress, by my body language, and by projecting less warmth from my personality. That goes against my very nature, but my need for protection dictated that changes be made.

Still, I did not want to assume sole responsibility for avoiding unwanted attention—especially since this was not the only man who had made me feel uncomfortable. "If you see me talking alone with any man for more than ninety seconds, I want you to come and stand beside me," I said to the women. "You don't need to join the conversation. Just be there so I can tap you on the shoulder if I need help."

Soon after the incident I moved from the area, so I could not judge the effectiveness of our combined efforts. Nevertheless, my experience taught me some valuable lessons that I took with me.

The Garbage Dump

Sometimes spending an hour in a counseling session is comparable to spending the same amount of time browsing in an adult book store. The sordid details some people feel compelled to confess equate with pornography. How can Christian leaders prevent being contaminated by the garbage dumped on them?

While I was on staff at a certain church, an unexpected turn of events put me in a situation where I was required to do extensive counseling. I heard about an extramarital affair, addiction to pornography, and perversion. Although I've always been able to separate work from play, too much exposure to graphic details started to affect me personally.

Date night with my husband lost its luster. When I kissed Kurt, I felt squeamish. Sensing the distance between us, Kurt asked, "Is something wrong?"

"No, I don't know what it is." All of a sudden anything that had to do with sex was perverted and dirty to me, but I didn't want to talk about it. I tried to straighten myself out. *Sex is a gift from God,* I kept telling myself, but I couldn't overcome the effects of my counseling sessions.

Finally Kurt said, "We need to talk about the problem."

After my attempt to explain my feelings, Kurt said, "In all our years of marriage this has never been a problem. Why is it now?"

"Because I hear nothing but the bad parts of it." In general terms I described some of what I was hearing.

"Why are you allowing people to tell you this?"

"I'm trying to bring healing to them."

Through my conversation with Kurt, I began to understand better what was happening. "They're sneezing on you, and you're coming down with pneumonia," he said. From Kurt I learned that instead of bringing healing, I was actually allowing individuals another outlet to express their depravity. "As they talk about sex, they like to dwell on the sordid details," he said. I realized some of the people I had counseled enjoyed reliving the past.

Determined not to let my job ruin my life, I appealed for help. Several changes were implemented. If I ran into difficulty, a male staff person came to my rescue. No longer did I close the door while counseling with a man. Support from the staff, an open door, and the cooperation of an alert secretary took care of the problem.

I have since learned how to take control as I deal with men who bring up the subject of sex. Because I'm aware of potential danger, I can squelch problems before they have a chance to develop.

After one of my sessions on the road, people lined up to talk with me. One man kept moving to the back of the line, and I realized he wanted to be alone with me.

His first question put me on the defensive. "Are you mature?" Before I could answer, he continued, "I need to share some things with you, but I want to know if you're mature.

"I'm mature, but I don't need graphic information," I said. "Generally, tell me your issue, and I will pray with you."

Somewhat stunned, he seemed to be at a loss for words. "If you don't feel you can share with me, that's fine," I said.

"No, I'll share with you. I struggle with women," he said.

"That's all I need to know. Let's pray."

As soon as I finished, he said, "What would you say if I told you I was a transvestite?"

"I would say the same thing I would say about any sexual sin. You need Jesus Christ, you need to get into accountability, and you need counseling. I appreciate the opportunity to pray with you, but if you need further assistance, I'm sure there are some strong men in this conference who can help you."

That approach probably benefited him more than if I had given him a sympathetic ear. It certainly was less traumatic for me.

Not only do Christian leaders need to safeguard their own emotions, they also need to discourage an emotional attachment by members of the opposite sex. Youth ministers are particularly vulnerable in this area. Impressionable young girls often pick up on the first friendly gesture. Lonely women also pose problems for male pastors who counsel with them.

There is a fine line between the healthy bond that forms from helping someone through a crisis and a relationship based on fleshly attraction. With the exercise of our best judgment and guidance from the Holy Spirit, we can stay on the safe side.

If you are single and aspire to Christian leadership, you probably endorse the biblical standard of sexual purity. In spite of good intentions, however, Christians sometimes allow passion to rule instead of prudence.

For Christians the problem does not usually arise on casual dates. As a relationship intensifies, so does the desire for physical contact. Engaged couples are particularly susceptible to temptation.

Couples who plan to go into ministry are at risk on two counts during courtship. Engaging in premarital sex reduces the chances of a happy marriage and becomes an enormous obstacle to effective ministry. One act of indiscretion can jeopardize the two things you most desire: marriage and ministry.

Reader Challenge

• I challenge singles to take an aggressive stand for sexual purity. When you pray, "Lead us not into temptation," do your part to help the Holy Spirit curb fleshly desire. Avoid situations that encourage transgression. Your entire future is on the line. How will you respond?

• Perhaps you are already involved in a leadership role. As you comfort someone who is hurting, do you ever become emotionally involved? How can you guard against this?

• Can your words or actions be interpreted as an invitation to get better acquainted?

• Do you struggle to maintain your own emotional health after exposure to real-life experiences involving sexual immorality? Trying to bring healing to someone in sexual sin by listening to sordid details is like wallowing in the mud with someone you hope to rescue from the mire.

• Write out how you will bring about changes needed to prevent Satan from bringing his version of sexuality into your sanctuary. You might feel the need to enlist someone or a group of people to hold you accountable in this area.

• Revise this prayer to fit your situation:

DEAR GOD, you were so wise in creating male and female. Thank you for the gift of sexuality, which is intended to bring fulfillment to the human experience. Forgive me for the times I have deviated from the biblical standard of purity in word, thought, or deed. Surround me and those I serve with the protecting power of the Holy Spirit. Rebuke Satan's influence from our sanctuary. In Jesus' name I pray. Amen.

CHAPTER 6

Voluntary Slaves

Some passages from Scripture capture my attention more than others. For instance, I get absolutely ecstatic when I read, "Where the Spirit of the Lord is, there is freedom" (2 Cor 3:17). Another verse seems to be written just for Lori Salierno: "Christ has set us free. Stand firm, therefore, and do not submit again to a yoke of slavery" (Gal 5:1).

I *love* freedom. Unless an activity is sinful or unhealthy, I want to be free to try it. My spirit of adventure has taken me trekking in the Himalayas and climbing to the summits of Mount Kilimanjaro and Mount Fugi. I've jumped with a parachute from an airplane and ridden an elephant in the jungle. Great fun! Who knows what I'll try next? Maybe an opportunity will open up to explore God's creativity in outer space.

People try to change me all the time. "Don't be so dramatic," they say. Or, "Don't talk to every stranger

you meet." Some people want to put me in a mold. I've even tried to fit in a mold, but I break out every time.

The one person who gives me total freedom is my husband, Kurt. Unless my safety or a Christian principle is at stake, Kurt says, "Go for it." His acceptance of me the way I am was one of the many reasons I became attracted to Kurt in the first place. "I don't want to detract from the person God made her to be," Kurt tells people who say he should clamp down on my unconventional style.

Just when I begin to feel comfortable with my sense of freedom, I read in the Bible, "Though I am free with respect to all, I have made myself a slave to all, so that I might win more of them" (1 Cor 9:19). How can I be free and be a slave at the same time? Even more important to me, why should I be a slave?

Voluntary Servitude

Although I dislike discipline imposed by others, I have the ability to regulate my own actions. With sufficient motive I can be quite severe on myself.

Nothing gives me stronger motivation than my love for Jesus Christ. If my devotion to Christ cools, I need but remind myself of what Christ did for me to ignite the flame of love in my heart. Until Jesus paid the price for my sins, eternal death awaited me. That is why the Apostle Paul wrote, "You are not your own; you were bought at a price" (1 Cor 6:19–20, NIV).

Because my Savior willingly suffered and died for me, I choose to become a slave for the gospel.

Even after making a commitment, my servitude does not come easily. Losing my individual freedom is painful to me regardless of the reason. The lack of clear-cut guidelines as to where freedom ends and slavery begins also poses a problem for me.

A Role Model

If I want to find an example of voluntary servitude, I need not look far. During his street ministry Kurt Salierno offered himself as a slave for Christ over and over again.[1]

Once Kurt was talking with a group of derelicts when a fight broke out. Scuffles were common, but that time the brawl escalated until the police intervened. Everyone present was arrested.

One of the officers knew Kurt and understood he played no role in the disturbance, but he wanted to discourage him from working the streets. Kurt ended up in a drunk tank with several others, including two men who did not live on skid row. They had gone there to buy cheap liquor and get drunk.

During the course of conversation Kurt had the opportunity to tell the men about Jesus and the changes Christ could make in people's lives. Many ignored him, and some became testy.

"If you really believe that, what are you doing here?" one man asked.

"I don't have to be here. I choose to be here because I love these people."

Surprised, the men wondered how anyone could love people who were wallowing in degradation. They berated themselves for their condition and vowed never again to get caught in a similar situation.

Kurt was ready with a reason for the love that surged through his heart. "I love these men because God gives me the kind of love Jesus had for people. Through God's eyes I don't see them as outcasts of society. Rather, I see them as they could be through Jesus Christ."

No one spoke for several minutes. Finally, one man said, "Do you see yourself doing any good?"

"Not often, but God has changed some lives of people on the streets. A few people have found a new beginning and hope of eternal life."

The silence that followed was broken by the sound of muffled sobs. In the dark room Kurt moved closer to the sound to find out what was happening. A man placed his hand on Kurt's and said, "I need something in my life. I look forward to weekends because I can't handle the pressures of work. Then on the weekends I can't handle my family. If you can give these guys on the street some hope, what about us who don't live here? We're just as messed up as they are."

That was all it took to excite Kurt. He explained to the men what Jesus Christ could do for them. In jail, both men accepted Jesus as Savior. Before they were released, Kurt said, "It won't be easy, but the Holy Spirit will be your teacher and your guide. Find a

Bible-believing church and begin sharing with others about the new life you have begun."

When Kurt was first jailed, he felt sorry for himself, almost to the point of anger. By the time he left, he hardly noticed the stench permeating the air. He was too busy rejoicing with the angels in heaven over two sinners who repented.

Erasing Question Marks

Sometimes slavery requires us to avoid a situation that raises questions. When I received an invitation to go to Africa to work with missionaries, Kurt approved the venture if I could find someone to go with me. A married woman and a single man in the congregation I attended volunteered to accompany me. I had known the man for a number of years, and we had a brother-sister relationship. Kurt found such an arrangement satisfactory.

I called the president of the missionary board responsible for my invitation. "There will be two married women and one single man going to Africa," I said. "Do you have a problem with that?"

"Does Kurt have a problem with it?"

"No."

"I don't either."

Based on the consent of those two men, I made the trip as planned. Almost as soon as we arrived in Africa someone remarked, "I'm surprised your husbands would allow their wives to travel with a single man."

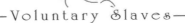
The comment caused me some consternation, but I didn't comprehend the significance of the situation until one of the missionaries explained. "The African people won't understand why two married women would travel with a single man," she said. "In their culture, a married woman would never go anywhere without her husband. A single man would travel with women only if they were his concubines."

What an indictment against a perfectly innocent arrangement! By then, of course, I was already there and couldn't change the circumstances. All I could do was try to cover the situation with a Band-aid. "I can see I should have learned more about the African culture before I made plans," I said. "Maybe the three of us will blend into the rest of the group, and it won't show up so much."

The experience taught me a lesson I took home with me. Not only must I ask, *Is this right or wrong?* I also must ask, *How will it appear to others?* A verse of Scripture I had often read took on new meaning: "Abstain from all appearance of evil" (1 Thess 5:22, KJV).

After deciding to be more careful in the future, I considered the matter to be closed. More than a year later I heard from two sources that people still questioned my actions. Question marks are hard to erase, but I need to keep them from coming up in the first place.

As much as I dislike living in a glass bowl, I realize that the more public exposure I receive the

less privacy I have. Therefore I must say with the Apostle Paul, " 'All things are lawful,' but not all things are beneficial. 'All things are lawful,' but not all things build up" (1 Cor 10:23).

I wish I had learned to be more careful about how actions appear before I experienced an embarrassing moment. When I had the privilege of meeting a prominent Christian leader I had long admired, I was so thrilled I wanted to have my picture taken with him. In my own amiable style I slipped my arm around his waist. Quite unobtrusively he took hold of my hand, brought it out front and said, "Why don't we do this?"

His manner was gracious, but I chided myself for failing to exercise discretion. More and more I must tell myself, *Think, Salierno, think!*

Personal Benefit

Some restrictions on behavior are for personal benefit. At the gym one day I was lifting weights and minding my own business when a man walked up to my bench and sat down beside me. In spite of the fact that I totally ignored him, he persisted in trying to strike up a conversation. "I feel it's my manly duty to tell you something," he said.

I stiffened. He made one comment that offended me, and I didn't want to hear more. When I didn't respond, he got up and walked away but continued to watch me. The whole incident made me uncomfortable, and I dreaded telling the women in my core group what happened.

"What were you wearing?" Shelley asked when I finished my story.

"My workout clothes."

"What do the workout clothes look like?"

As soon as she asked, I realized I was partly to blame for an unpleasant experience, but I wasn't quite ready to admit it. Somewhat defensively I said, "Well, Shelley, I wasn't wearing anything that other women don't wear."

"I didn't ask what they were wearing. What were you wearing?"

Ouch! My system of accountability actually called for a straightforward approach, and here I was weaseling around the questions. In a meek tone of voice I said, "I was wearing a body suit. It was tight, but when I go to the gym, I don't talk to men. I work out for forty-five minutes, and I'm out of there."

"Then don't be surprised if men say this kind of thing to you. Whether you like it or not, men will notice when you wear that kind of an outfit."

After hearing about the incident, Kurt said, "I'll be going to the gym with you the next time."

In my baggy shorts with my husband by my side, I felt much safer. The same man came up to me and said, "Who's the new guy?"

Kurt stepped forward and said, "My name's Kurt—her husband." The man backed off immediately and didn't bother me after that.

Defining Modesty

It's one thing to wear sloppy clothes to the gym but quite another to adopt the dowdy look as a mode of dress. I like fashion. The way I dress is an expression of who I am. I'm not a conventional type of person, and that comes through in my choice of clothes.

Perhaps the independent part of me conflicts with my role in ministry. I can relate to Ruth Stafford Peale, wife of the late Dr. Norman Vincent Peale— pastor to thousands, loved by millions. Growing up in a pastor's home, Miss Stafford wanted no part of marrying a minister. Among her reasons: "When dresses are short, I want mine as short as anyone else's."[2] Well, Mrs. Peale did all right, and so maybe there is hope for me.

Only hours before I was to speak to a large convention, someone objected to what I was going to wear. Because my knees would show, I was told, "Some of the older ladies will be turned off, and some of the younger men will be turned on." Previous experience told me the argument regarding younger men had validity, but it was too late to change plans.

After I finished speaking, my critic complimented me, and I asked, "Well, how did the dress go?"

"You were saved by a row of plants all across the front of the platform. No one could see your knees; so we both won." If the Lord arranged for the plants to protect me in spite of myself, what about next time?

God's Word is the authority on any issue. Regarding dress, the Bible says, "The women should dress themselves modestly and decently in suitable clothing" (1 Tim 2:9). The question is: How do we define modesty and decency?

Inside Religion

As I pondered the answer to a difficult question, I began to wonder how others in my position handled the issue of dress. Ann Denton was a popular speaker in her day and was the first person to inspire me (as a five-year-old child) to go into ministry. Her picture in a 1931 yearbook showed her to be quite fashionable, and I had read that she was a "flashy dresser."

The story had been told that a woman once approached Mrs. Denton after she finished speaking. "I liked your message, but do you know, honey, I could see your elbows."

"I'm sorry if that offended you. If you will let me know when you're going to be in the audience, I will see to it that my elbows are covered," she had replied in a lighthearted manner.

Mrs. Denton confirmed the story was true. That was so many years ago. We surely don't have people living like that any more, do we?

Well, not exactly. At least we have shifted from elbows to knees.

Looking back at her early ministry, Mrs. Denton wondered how she survived. In those days long hair was in; jewelry and makeup were out. How did she survive?

"I never let criticism become a burden to me. If I could, I'd turn it around to laugh it off. In fact, I've often said if I didn't have a sense of humor, I wouldn't have any sense at all."

That was the Ann Denton I remembered—always handy with the one-liners.

Red was one of her favorite colors, and she wore it often. "Don't you know that red is the devil's color?" a lady once said to her.

"I don't know that much about the devil, but he must have good taste," Mrs. Denton replied.

One situation, however, called for a more serious response. A woman sat down beside the speaker, pulled a tissue from her purse and wiped it across Mrs. Denton's lips. Holding up the tissue tinged with red, the woman exclaimed in triumph, "I *knew* you had on lipstick."

Although somewhat nonplussed, Mrs. Denton had a ready reply. In a modulated tone of voice she said, "Fortunately for you, I wear my religion on the inside instead of on the outside. If you had done that to the old Ann Denton before the Lord got hold of her, you would have gotten your face slapped."

I like the emphasis on inside religion. Unless our Christian experience goes beyond the surface, we will never be effective leaders, no matter how much we please people. Submission to the dictates of others will not take the place of a heart that is right with God.

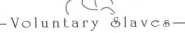
Biblical Guidelines

Although I can gain insight from other people, I must make my own decisions based on Scripture regarding when I am free and when I am a slave. Romans 14:21 provides a good test to determine whether or not I have the freedom to do a certain thing. "It is good not to ... do anything that makes your brother or sister stumble." Jesus made an even stronger case. "Occasions for stumbling are bound to come, but woe to the one by whom the stumbling block comes!" (Matt 18:7). Like it or not, I am responsible for how my actions affect others.

According to 1 Corinthians 10:23, we need to focus on that which builds up. That poses somewhat of a conflict for me regarding the dress issue. If I want the gospel message to be heard by students, I need to wear the uniform of youth. If I don't, they will turn me off immediately. At the same time a youthful image may offend older women or give the wrong message to men. That causes me to walk a fine line, and I'm still trying to find my way.

Another gauge of conduct comes from Galatians 5:13: "You were called to freedom, brothers and sisters; only do not use your freedom as an opportunity for self-indulgence, but through love become slaves to one another." If I am motivated by love, I am willing to become a slave when it means freedom for others. The spiritual welfare of my brothers and sisters will take precedence over my own desires.

All of these guidelines combined do not always give me a definite answer. For me, the bottom line is based on whether or not God gives me a sense of peace concerning anything that is subject to question. As long as I'm surrendered to God's will, I can count on the Holy Spirit to convict me if I should change my thinking.

When someone criticizes something I do, I need to pay attention to all of the guidelines above, and I need to pray, "Lord, I don't have a problem with it, but if this will cause someone to fall, create within me an impression of what I should do." If I'm sincere when I pray, I need to listen for the Holy Spirit's voice in order to receive direction.

Easy Answers

Some issues that plague other people don't bother me at all. For instance, I totally abstain from alcohol and have no desire to indulge in even a social drink.

I grew up under the teaching that even temperate use of alcohol was sin, but I don't believe the doctrine has a solid biblical base. Most of the Scriptures dealing with wine and strong drink warn against drunkenness and excess indulgence, thus supporting temperance but not necessarily total abstinence. In fact, Paul wrote to Timothy, "No longer drink only water, but take a little wine for the sake of your stomach and your frequent ailments" (1 Tim 5:23).

In an attempt to explain examples of biblical approval of the use of wine, such as when Jesus turned water into wine at a wedding, some people argue that the wine was merely grape juice. Neither biblical nor secular history supports this view. Furthermore, if wine had no potential for intoxication, the Bible would have placed no restrictions on its use, whatsoever.

If, however, I look at the matter from the standpoint of expediency rather than legality, I arrive at a different conclusion. I don't want to risk leading others astray. What I could do in moderation, others might do in excess.

In my work with youth the drug scene is a big issue. If I took a social drink, how could I influence young people to stay off drugs? It's the same thing, kids say, and they have a point. Could I honestly differentiate between a cocktail, a cigarette, and cocaine?

A strong personal stand against alcohol does not allow me to brand as sinners all those whose convictions differ from mine. In this regard I will do well to follow the biblical injunction against judgment of others.

The Price Tag

Anything worthwhile carries a price tag. If we want to be effective leaders, we must assume the role of the servant or slave. Sometimes that may come easily. At other times servanthood will cause us pain. We may be stepped on, pinched, punched, or knocked down. When that happens to me, I fight like crazy. I don't want anyone tampering with what I consider to be my rights.

When I begin to fight for my rights, however, I must ask myself, *What rights?* Did I not surrender my rights to Jesus Christ when I committed my life to him? Did not the price he paid for my sins buy my personal rights as well? Suddenly my impulse to fight falters.

Does that mean I must follow the dictates of everyone who wants to change my style? No. I relinquished my rights to Jesus Christ, not to human lords. Servanthood does mean I will evaluate human advice and ask God if it has relevance for me.

Sometimes the answer is no; sometimes it is yes. Even though the yes answers hurt, I am still the winner if I make the required adjustments. Every time I surrender my will to God's will I gain spiritual strength to help me keep my life and ministry on track. If I want to go full distance with God, I must do it one day at a time. Unless I meet the challenge of each day, I cannot progress beyond my present level of maturity.

Losing some of my personal freedom is a small price to pay to become a full partner in Christ's mission on earth. Eternal consequences will more than make up for any sacrifice I am called to make.

Reader Challenge

• Is freedom a top priority to you as it is to me? Do you rebel when others try to restrict your freedom? In what area do you struggle? Consider such possibilities as dress, alcohol, tobacco, television, movies, gossip, or careless language. What does the Bible say about your struggle?

• Does the freedom you claim as your right pose a stumbling block to others? Does it build up God's kingdom or tear it down? Do you use your freedom to indulge selfish interest?

• Will the questionable activity bring you under its control? If so, would you rather be a slave to your own desires than to be a servant of Jesus Christ?

• Do any of your actions leave question marks as to whether or not your behavior is appropriate? Are you willing to take the necessary steps to erase the question marks?

• Will you indenture yourself as a slave to Christ in one particular area? Confirm your pledge with a prayer:

DEAR GOD, thank you for my freedom in Christ that took away my sins and promises eternal life. Thank you for giving me a unique personality duplicated in no other individual. Sometimes, though, my independent nature conflicts with my desire to be a slave for the sake of the gospel. Help me to measure the criticism that comes from others with divine instruments. Give me the courage to crucify my flesh when necessary. Lord, I recognize your majesty and realize you can control my life far better than I. Therefore, I fall at your feet as your slave for Jesus' sake. Amen.

1. Salierno, 25–29.
2. Quote from movie, *One Man's Way*. Permission to include quote granted by Ruth Stafford Peale in October 20, 1995 letter.

CHAPTER 7

The Clay Jar Image

The scene looks strangely familiar. A darkened auditorium ... dancing lights directed toward the stage ... thousands of enthusiastic fans. The fans go wild as a popular Christian music group testifies through song to the power of the Word of God. I have not attended one of the concerts performed by the group before, but I feel as though I am watching a rerun of a movie.

Where have I seen this picture before? I ask myself. Then I remember. Six months earlier I had treated as fantasy the vision of taking the gospel to America West Arena in Phoenix. I can hardly believe that fantasy has turned to reality in a few short months.

Checking the time, I realize the spotlight will soon shift to me. Will I be able to hold the audience in rapt attention as the recording artists are now doing? More importantly, will my message penetrate the hearts of the listeners? As my mind reflects on the task that lies before me, my flesh tingles as my lips whisper: "Lord, who am I to assume such an awesome responsibility?"

I do not listen for God's answer because I do not expect to receive a reply. I'm too busy analyzing the happenings of each moment. So it takes me by surprise when God interrupts my thoughts. As clearly as though a voice boomed from heaven, God speaks to me, "It's not about who you are; it's about who I am."

How could I have forgotten? How can I forget the verse from Scripture I often repeat? "We have this treasure in clay jars, so that it may be made clear that this extraordinary power belongs to God and does not come from us" (2 Cor 4:7).

Lord, Lord, remove Lori Salierno from the spotlight. Replace her with a clay jar empowered by your Holy Spirit.

The Focal Point

It's difficult for me to evaluate myself regarding humility; so I won't even try. If I ever come to the place where I think I'm humble, I probably won't be. Self-manufactured humility can actually be a form of arrogance. As long as I focus on myself, self-analysis will be distorted.

Only as I shift my focal point to God can I begin to build a clay jar image. Recognizing the majesty of God helps me to see myself in proper perspective. I am merely mortal, yet the God who commands the

universe chooses to show divine power through me! Any good that comes from my ministry is God's doing, not mine.

If people respond to the invitation to accept Jesus as their Savior, it is only through the Holy Spirit. When I went with an evangelistic team to Estonia, I was asked to speak in the closing service. Because I was mentally and physically exhausted, I asked the Lord for an extra measure of strength.

Almost as soon as I began to speak I felt renewed energy, and the Holy Spirit moved in mighty power. A few individuals responded immediately to the altar call. As the pull of the Holy Spirit grew stronger, people began to flock to the altar. I'm always thrilled to see anyone come to the Lord, but even more so if I have pointed the way. While people continued to come, I began to feel somewhat like Billy Graham must have felt during his many evangelistic campaigns.

Although my mind made reference to Billy Graham facetiously, I can learn much from the renowned evangelist. Through decades of successful ministry, Dr. Graham has remained a humble servant of God. I can never hope to equal Dr. Graham's impact on the kingdom of heaven. If he can keep his focus on God at his success level, how can I take personal credit for the results of my efforts?

One of the highlights of my ministry is hearing testimonies of students who have decided to remain sexually pure or dedicate their lives to ministry. As I rejoice over life-changing decisions, I must realize that my message did not make the difference. Without input from the Holy Spirit my words are empty.

Dealing with Praise

When the Holy Spirit works through a Christian leader, those who are helped often honor the leader. In spite of the case for humility I must admit I enjoy receiving accolades. Because I'm extremely extroverted I love attention. Does enjoyment of positive feedback rule out the possibility of my building a clay jar image?

It could, but I don't believe it will irresistibly deprave me. It probably means I will need to work at keeping myself in perspective. I will need some balance for a personality trait that basks in receiving attention.

If I consider myself as being in partnership with the Lord and remember I am only the junior partner, I will be more likely to turn the spotlight from me to God. Although I enjoy sharing center stage, I will extend the credit for the performance to my Senior Partner.

In dealing with accolades tossed my way, I want to be guided by the words of the Apostle Paul: "May I never boast of anything except the cross of our Lord Jesus Christ, by which the world has been crucified to me, and I to the world" (Gal 6:14).

Role Model in Humility

While we cannot accurately judge ourselves in regard to humility, we can gain considerable value from recognizing humility in others. We tend to cultivate in ourselves the traits we admire in someone else.

In many ways Mother Teresa is a role model to me. If I were to choose one of her qualities I would most like to emulate, it would probably be her humble spirit.

The first time a group of students and I went to India to work in Mother Teresa's homes, we did not have the opportunity to meet her until we went to the airport for our return flight. During that meeting she asked each person in the group, "Did you enjoy the work?" Her follow-up question probed even deeper into our commitment, "Did you give until it hurt?"

During a return trip to India our group had the privilege of working with Mother Teresa on three occasions. Everything she did demonstrated her joy in sacrificial giving.

In the home for mentally challenged children Mother Teresa did not assume a supervisory role. She tended to the same mundane duties we did—feeding the children, folding laundry, or just soothing a hurting child with a tender touch. Some of the children were unable to even acknowledge her presence, but that did not diminish the joy of the saintly woman.

To Mother Teresa job satisfaction is based on faithfulness in service rather than on success as defined by the world. "God didn't call me to be successful," she has stated. "God simply called me to be faithful."

Little acts of kindness excite the woman who heads an international organization called the Missionaries of Charity. While we visited the Mother House where Mother Teresa lives, a load of blankets arrived for distribution among prostitutes. Donated by the Hindu community, the blankets represented a spirit of caring and cooperation that crossed religious boundaries.

As my brother, Bob, unloaded the blankets, Mother Teresa's face glowed with joy. "This never happens," she repeated several times. Even after the blankets were stacked in place, she continued to marvel at the wonder of receiving such a gift.

"Come, sit, talk," she said to my brother and a few others in our group. "Tell me about your ministry." Then the woman who could command an audience anywhere in the world listened with rapt attention and encouraging words as members of the group described their areas of service.

What keeps this diminutive, energetic woman going? While Christians everywhere talk about the power of prayer, Mother Teresa's life demonstrates the value of spending four hours each day with God. At nearly ninety years of age, she prays on her knees for a full hour at a time. I was privileged to join her in

prayer on one occasion, and was blessed by the simplicity and sincerity of her communion with God.

Mother Teresa encourages her co-workers to pray often throughout the day. The guide she provides for daily prayer calls for a spirit of humility and focuses on the need to extend comfort, love, understanding, and forgiveness to others. I fully appreciate her approach to prayer.

Solicited Counsel

Attitudes of the heart determine whether we come across as humble or haughty. We shape our attitudes through direct communion with God, but those who are close to us can point out behavior that indicates the need for an attitude adjustment.

Accountability partners or close associates can better help us build a clay jar image if they have specific permission to do so. People may hesitate to point out what they perceive to be an arrogant attitude for fear we may not be open to suggestion.

On our accountability sheet we might include questions designed to reveal any tendency toward self-importance. For example: What have you observed in my actions that comes across as arrogant? By indicating we expect to receive advice in this area, we allow our accountability partners freedom to share their opinions.

At times we might invite input regarding a specific situation: Did I sound egotistical when I...? How could I handle a similar situation next time?

The simple act of making ourselves vulnerable to admonition is a good start toward building a clay jar image. We will watch our attitudes more closely if we know they will be evaluated.

Insight from Critics

Unsolicited advice can be quite painful. It often sounds like someone wants to destroy us rather than help us.

In his book about the life and principles of Dr. James Dobson, Rolf Zettersten devotes an entire chapter to "Common Criticisms." Zettersten writes, "Even at a rate of two negative letters per thousand, that means he receives more than four hundred written comments every month from people who are upset about something. Some offer constructive criticism. Others take off his hide."[1]

From my calculations Dr. Dobson receives 20,000 letters each month—far more than I hope to receive in a lifetime. Although 19,600 of the letters are positive in tone, the 400 negative letters concern him most.

Zettersten writes, "After reading the accumulated responses of his critics each month, Dobson says he feels as though he has been hit with a two-by-four about four hundred times. The most painful criticism, of course, is that which we recognize as valid indicators of ministry weakness."[2]

I don't receive that volume of mail, but I felt as though I had been hit with several two-by-fours from receiving one particular letter. A lady who had heard

me speak once, maybe twice, wrote me a lengthy letter filled with criticism. She didn't like the size of my Bible, the way I pointed my finger, or the way I interpreted Scripture. Most of all she didn't like my stories and accused me of setting myself up as a spiritual guru when I needed a lot of work myself. On and on she went, concluding with, "You should sit down and shut up!"

After reading the letter, I was totally devastated. I didn't have my accountability partners then, and so I called my dad.

"Are any of those accusations true?" he asked.

"I definitely think my message is based on God's Word. I do tell stories about myself, but I don't mean to set myself up as a perfect example. I know one thing, I can't sit down and shut up because God has called me to stand up and speak out."

After a moment of thought, my dad said, "Keep anything relevant and apply it. Then forget about the rest."

Based on that conversation I decided to be more careful about relating personal experiences. I tend to weed out my failures and share my successes, but I asked God to help me include stories that reveal my shortcomings. If I make myself vulnerable, I can then show how God is working with me to overcome human weakness.

I did not respond to the lady who wrote the letter. It might have been well to reply with a letter like this:

Thank you for taking your time to write to me. I assume your comments were intended to help me become more effective in ministry, which gives us a common goal. In working toward that goal, however, I sometimes experience pain. When I read your remark indicating I misrepresent Scripture, I agonized inside because I cherish God's Word. If you will give me examples of where I am in error, I will gladly reevaluate my position through prayer and extensive Bible study.

I don't mean to focus the spotlight on me, but I find that many people identify with my narrative style of preaching. Perhaps I'm guilty of telling my success stories while being lax in relating my failures, which are many. Thank you for pointing that out to me, and I will try to take corrective action in the future.

Even if it seems our critics are trying to ruin our ministry, we can soften the impact of the accusations by building a bridge of friendship. Rally the other person to our side. The preceding letter does that with the sentence: "I assume your comments were intended to help me become more effective in ministry, which gives us a common goal."

Rather than become defensive over petty issues (such as the size of my Bible or the way I point my finger), it is better to focus on significant allegations. Invite further dialogue to clarify any ambiguous statements. For instance, "Show me examples of where I am out of line with Scripture."

Notice also that the letter does not blame my critic for my distress. No one causes us to have certain feelings; we choose them ourselves. Thus, the letter states the feelings I had when I was accused of poor Bible interpretation, but the accuser is not blamed for the feelings I had.

Perhaps the most important step in building a bridge of friendship is to indicate appreciation for the value received from the communication. In my case, I promised to balance my success stories with accounts of my failures.

When we choose to respond to a letter of criticism, we should wait until our emotions have settled down. As long as we feel the sting of sharp words, it's hard to be objective. Prayer will help us develop a soft answer that will mellow the hearts of our accusers as well as our own. By properly processing criticism, we can benefit from that which is helpful and reject that which is harmful.

The Motivating Factor

How we function in any situation depends largely upon what motivated our involvement in the first place. The very nature of ministry seems to rule out our usual notions of motivation. We all know that, generally speaking, ministry-related careers do not offer massive financial compensation. Neither can many religious leaders expect to gain fame or power.

It is usually in response to Christ's Great Commission that individuals dedicate their leadership ability to ministry. Especially in the beginning they feel a calling that sends them forth with a divine purpose.

When Jesus taught the disciples after washing their feet, he provided the key to building a clay jar image. He told those disciples in the upper room, "I give you a new commandment, that you love one another. Just as I have loved you, you also should love one another. By this everyone will know that you are my disciples, if you have love for one another" (John 13:34–35).

To illustrate that kind of love I can think of no better example than a man named Max, who lived on skid row in Portland, Oregon, while my husband, Kurt, ministered there.[3]

Max was more receptive to Kurt's message than most of the men on the streets. The two men talked about Jesus for several days as Max's interest mounted. Finally, Max asked the question Kurt prayed to hear: "Is it too late for me to have that eternal life and joy?"

After praying with Max on the sidewalk, Kurt said to his new brother in the Lord, "In the same way that Christ loved us, Christ wants us to love others."

The words sounded almost routine to Kurt because he had said them to many people who accepted Jesus, but Max responded with enthusiasm. "Christ wants us to love others just as he loves us," he repeated over and over.

During winter nights those who were fortunate found a place in the shelter. One time Max and Kurt had the opportunity to go into a shelter, but Max allowed others to go in ahead of him. He said to Kurt, "Jesus would do that, wouldn't he?"

Kurt hardly knew how to respond because he was so cold, but he agreed Max was right. They spent the night in an alley huddled together with others for warmth. Max placed himself on the outer edge to protect the others.

One morning, after a severely cold night, Max did not rise to his feet as the others did. Yet he had a smile on his face. "We made it, didn't we? That was one of the toughest storms I have ever been in, but we made it." His joy came from knowing he had taken the vulnerable position so that others might be warmed by his body.

"Come on, let's get some coffee," Kurt said.

Max gestured for Kurt to come closer. "You need to help me. I can't feel my feet," he said.

Kurt removed Max's shoes that were covered with ice. His feet were white from frost-bite. Summoning a policeman, Kurt requested help for his friend.

After a short hospital stay Max was back on the street, but his feet were bandaged.

"What happened, Max?" Kurt asked.

"They took them off. They took my toes off."

"Max, I am so sorry."

"I'm okay, Kurt. It's just like what Jesus did. Don't be sorry for me. It's a joy to be able to do this for you guys."

Gangrene set in, and Max had to have his legs amputated just below the knees. Tragedy did not diminish his smile or curtail his joy in the Lord.

The gangrene spread, and Max died in the hospital. From reports, Kurt learned that Max had remained full of joy and talked about Jesus to the end.

When I think of Max, a prayer forms in the depths of my soul: *Lord, help me to love like Max.*

The Anointing

A pastor called a young minister to hold a series of meetings. The young man I'll call Timothy (not his real name) was an extremely effective communicator who made people in his audience feel as though they had received a message from God.

Recognizing the pressures that tend to pull talented ministers in different directions, the pastor said to Timothy, "Whatever you do, don't ever lose the anointing." Through more than two decades of successful ministry Timothy followed that advice.

The Old Testament first refers to the anointing as a means to consecrate Aaron and his sons as priests (Exod 30:30). Kings were anointed with oil as a symbol of God's appointment: Saul (1 Sam 10:1), David (1 Sam 16:13), and Solomon (1 Kings 1:39), but Saul lost the anointing through disobedience (1 Sam 15:24). Before his death Elijah the prophet anointed Elisha as his successor (1 Kings 19:16).

The anointing oil in the Old Testament symbolizes the Holy Spirit in the New Testament. We maintain the anointing of the Lord only as we open our hearts to receive the Holy Spirit—that part of God operating in our dispensation of time.

When we are anointed by the Holy Spirit, Satan will work harder to bring us down. If people are blessed by our efforts, the enemy will whisper, "You're pretty good, aren't you?" Satan will try to get us to claim credit for ideas inspired by the Holy Spirit.

If we want to build a clay jar image, we need to censure Satan's voice every time he suggests that perhaps God couldn't get along without us. When tempted by the devil in the wilderness, even Jesus said, "Away with you, Satan!" (Matt 4:10). Wanting to make a strong point, one man testified, "I told the devil to go to hell and stay there!"

Unless we remember our dependence upon God, seek divine guidance, and remain on constant guard against Satan, we will lose the anointing of the Holy Spirit.

"We have this treasure in clay jars, so that it may be made clear that this extraordinary power belongs to God and does not come from us" (2 Cor 4:7). We are mere clay jars with or without the treasure—the anointing of the Holy Spirit. On our own we will crumble and return to dust. With the anointing we can participate in demonstrating the extraordinary power of God.

Reader Challenge

• Do you vision yourself as a clay jar—a mere shell to house God's power?

• To create a more vivid picture, cut out a

facsimile of a clay jar from a brown paper grocery bag or equivalent. Write out 2 Corinthians 4:7, putting your name in place of the words *we* and *us*. *Have,* of course, will become *has.* Sample: "Lori has this treasure in a clay jar, so that it may be made clear that this extraordinary power belongs to God and does not come from her." Doesn't that make your flesh tingle? Keep the verse in a prominent place and refer to it often—especially after you have experienced unusual success.

• Will you commit to remaining faithful to your calling during times of discouragement as well as when all goes well? Choose one of the following Scriptures as your motto and etch it into your mind:

"It is required that those who have been given a trust must prove faithful" (1 Cor 4:2, NIV).

"Well done, good and faithful servant! You have been faithful with a few things; I will put you in charge of many things" (Matt 25:21, NIV).

• Will you solicit someone to help you build a clay jar image? With that person try role-playing your response to criticism.

• Do you love as Jesus loved? Do you love as Max loved? When you find your supply of love is weak, ask God to give you the kind of love demonstrated by Jesus.

• As you pray consider altering your posture from your usual position. Postures suggested in Scripture are bowing (Gen 24:26), kneeling (Ps 95:6), lying prostrate (Deut 9:25), and standing (1 Kings 8:22). No one posture offers a magic formula for reaching

God, but variety sometimes helps us express the depth of our desire to receive a fresh touch from God.

• Regularly pray the prayer printed below, especially when things are going well.

> ALMIGHTY GOD, thank you for choosing to place your treasure within me. Help me never to abuse or take credit for a demonstration of power by the Holy Spirit. May I always turn my laurels back to you. Teach me humility through my critics. God, in my humanness, I can never match your divine love, but help me to keep trying to express more and more of the love Jesus has for me. Anoint me with the Holy Spirit for your service. In Christ's name I pray. Amen.

1. Rolf Zettersten, *Dr. Dobson: Turning Hearts Toward Home* (Dallas, Texas: Word Publishing, 1989), 126.
2. ibid., 128.
3. Salierno, 11–16.

CHAPTER 8

Unbecoming Behaviors

For most of us the older we get the more we become creatures of habit. That which brought us pleasure once will bring us pleasure again, and so we repeat the performance until it becomes second nature. In so doing we run the risk of becoming slaves to undesirable behavior patterns. Before we realize what has happened, we are controlled by what gives us pleasure or satisfaction rather than by the Holy Spirit.

To do our best for God we need to develop well-balanced personalities. Excesses in any area of our lives can hinder our effectiveness in ministry. This is very obvious when repeated behaviors reflect poorly on the norms of Christian life and testimony. The following forms of behaviors represent problem areas for many leaders.

Improper Language

Some people who have the ugly habit of swearing don't realize what they are saying. A pastor in Tempe,

Arizona, worked with two men the congregation had hired to repair the roof of the sanctuary. One man used profane terms two or three times in every sentence, even when he wasn't angry.

In the heat of the day the man's partner asked, "Would you like a beer?"

The man who had desecrated the Lord's name countless times that day said, "A beer? With a preacher around! You have to be kidding."

When people whose speech is peppered with profanity become Christians, they often have difficulty cleaning up their vocabulary. It takes real effort to break the language barrier to spiritual growth, but it can be done.

A young lady I'll call Beth (not her real name) had been a Christian for a number of years, but she was not moving ahead in her Christian experience. Her path eventually crossed with that of a woman who saw great leadership potential in Beth.

Although Beth did not blaspheme God's name, she did punctuate her conversation with emphatic expressions and words bordering on profanity. According to Jesus, our manner of speech calls for extreme caution. "On the day of judgment you will have to give an account for every careless word you utter; for by your words you will be justified, and by your words you will be condemned" (Matt 12:36–37).

Acting as a mentor, the woman suggested that Beth weed out the offensive words from her vocabulary. After surrendering her life completely to

God, Beth tried to correct her faulty language, but often slipped up.

"Let's team up to get results," the woman offered. "I'll remind you every time I hear a word that's off-limits, and you'll owe me twenty bucks."

"That scares me, but I'll give it a try," Beth said.

For a few months the woman collected enough money to help support a Christian radio program. Then one day the woman complained of stiffness in her neck and shoulders.

"Tell me where it hurts, and I'll give you a massage," Beth said. As Beth gently massaged the affected area, she heard a popping sound and feared she might have injured the woman. Without thinking, Beth expressed her dismay with strong words.

"Twenty bucks!"

"That does it! No more money from me. You'll have to find another way to support your radio program." With that last twenty-dollar bill Beth decided to shape up before she went broke.

Because she held herself accountable in this and other areas, Beth began to move forward spiritually. Today the talented young woman is involved in Christian service in her local church as well as on a state level.

Twisted Truth

The four Gospels record Christ as saying, "I tell you the truth," more than seventy-five times. With Jesus as an example, surely Christian leaders want to

stick with the truth. Sometimes, however, truth spells trouble.

For instance, truth can hurt other people. In some cases truth can jeopardize our own safety or the safety of others. We need to be creative to avoid disaster while preserving truth.

A woman who lived alone became concerned for her safety because of certain happenings in her neighborhood. When she received a phone call from a man who said he was taking a survey, her mind waved a caution flag.

"Do you live alone?" the caller asked.

"No," she said, "my Father and my Brother live here with me." She answered truthfully because God is her Father and Jesus is her Brother.

Often we are tempted to twist truth to get out of a jam or to avoid getting into one. When my husband, Kurt, was in his teens, he faced severe repercussions if his account of current happenings did not please the authority figures in his life. He took the easy way out and simply revised the facts to reflect what would gain their approval.

Before long Kurt could hardly distinguish between truth and falsehood. At the same time that his troubles mounted because he began to tell conflicting stories, God brought him under conviction through Scripture. He read: "Therefore, putting away falsehood, let every one speak the truth" (Eph 4:25, RSV).

Kurt declared all-out war to break the control Satan had on his life. Not only did he have to learn to recognize truth, he had to learn new methods of dealing with authority. The battle was fierce, but with the help of the Holy Spirit and the prayers and encouragement of Christian friends Kurt gained victory over habitual lying.

As illustrated by the following true story (names have been changed), one untruth can cause irreparable damage.

It suddenly looked as though Harold Hines had it made. Without a college education he seemed headed toward owning his own business before age thirty. On the flight to work out the deal with Mr. Nelson, who offered him the opportunity, Harold envisioned a bright future.

Mr. Nelson showed Harold around the plant, then said, "By the way, Harold, what reason did you give your boss for being gone today?"

"I told him I was going to see my dad."

After a moment of reflection, Mr. Nelson said, "No, Harold, we don't lie in business. We don't always want to tell everything we know, but we don't lie." Mr. Nelson called off the deal because he feared Harold didn't have what it took to handle customers properly.

If what seems like a harmless fib can destroy a business career, how will a lie affect the ministry of Christian leaders? What might a preacher's prevarication in one situation say about his or her truthfulness in another circumstance?

Food Addiction

A most difficult compulsive behavior to deal with is the tendency to overeat. After all, it's impossible to live by a total just-say-no rule regarding food. Besides, all bodies are not created equally. Some people can continuously gorge themselves on food and never gain an ounce. The obstacles to dieting are great enough to cause many people to indulge their appetites without restraint.

Before joining my core group in Phoenix, Amanda had nearly given up trying to break the stronghold food had on her life. The result did not please her, but what could she do about it?

Nevertheless, Amanda felt a need to move closer to the Lord. Her pursuit of spiritual stature, however, was about as effective as her attempt at dieting. She wondered if she could win at anything.

One day Amanda sat on the couch in her den praying—actually pleading with God to send her a message through the Holy Spirit. Only the sound of the furnace droned in reply. In frustration, Amanda allowed her eyes to drift around the room as though searching for a sign from God.

Her eyes suddenly stopped moving as she focused on a book that seemed to hold her gaze with something like magnetic attraction. The book had been given to her some time before. Without even thumbing through the pages, Amanda had placed the book on a shelf and put it out of her mind. *Why does the book grip my mind so strongly now?* she asked herself.

Amanda removed the book from the shelf to examine it more closely. The title formed a prayer: *Help, Lord, the Devil Wants Me Fat.*[1] Could that be a suggestion from the Holy Spirit in how she should pray?

Of course not, Amanda decided as she tried to put the book away. What difference would her weight make to God or the devil?

Still, she could not part with the book. Opening it, she started to read. She had not read far when she began to think, *This is crazy.* No sooner had the idea formed in her mind than the words of the text told her exactly what she was thinking. Fascinated, she continued reading.

According to the author of the book, Satan controlled people's minds through their addiction to food. To break that control, the author suggested a ten-day fast, eliminating everything but water from the diet.

The concept was too bizarre for Amanda even to consider. With her medical problem, fasting was out of the question. Hypoglycemia requires a regular intake of nourishment. Returning the book to the shelf, Amanda vowed to forget the whole thing, but she couldn't. Every time she engaged her brain with another subject, her mind flipped back to the book.

When her husband came home, Amanda discussed her experience with him. She expected him to confirm her feeling that the idea was ridiculous.

Silence indicated he was giving the matter some thought. "Maybe you got a word from God," he finally ventured.

"But I've never fasted for even one meal in my life. Besides, it's too dangerous with hypoglycemia."

"Not if the Lord is in it."

For several days Amanda wrestled with indecision. Encouraged by her husband and sensing God's direction, she finally decided to take the challenge. Before stepping out on faith, though, she made preparations. She put together a prayer team for spiritual support and arranged to pick up a vitamin supplement especially designed for fasting. On the way to pick up the vitamins, Amanda had a car accident. Satan seemed intent on defeating her, but that only intensified her determination.

As time neared to start her fast, members of her prayer team began to call her with words of encouragement and promises from Scripture. One verse seemed to be written just for Amanda: "I tell you, the devil will ... test you, and you will suffer persecution for ten days" (Rev 2:10, NIV).

Although Amanda's medical condition required her to consume fruit juices the last five days, she completed the fast on her birthday with a sense of victory. "In a way I had two birthdays," she said. "One symbolized a new birth in my way of thinking about food. The experience transformed my life."

Of course, that initial encounter, as life-changing as it was, did not end Amanda's struggle. The motivation received from a dramatic experience can quickly subside without a program of regular discipline. Some people need to fight against food addiction every day of their lives.

At the right time Amanda joined the accountability group. The other women applauded even minor progress and offered words of encouragement when the going got tough. Karen and Jane kept her informed of the medical benefits of weight control. All the women prayed for Amanda as they did for each member of the group.

Amanda's experience tells us that even our food intake comes under the umbrella of accountability. Physically fit bodies are ideal temples to house the Holy Spirit. Keeping in shape can also enhance the effectiveness of our ministry. If our appearance demonstrates a disciplined lifestyle, we become an example that others will want to emulate.

Alcohol and Drugs

During the two years of his street ministry in Portland, Oregon, Kurt Salierno gained an extensive education in the effects of alcohol and drugs.[2] Repeatedly he heard stories of men who had once been successful in business but began to drink too much. Before long, alcohol took complete control of their lives, and they chose the refuge of skid row, where drunkenness was normal and acceptable.

Christian leaders who can handle a social drink would do well to share some of Kurt's experiences. If they could see the pain in Duke's eyes and hear the sadness in his voice as he told his story, they might want to revise their convictions regarding the use of alcohol. If they could witness Duke's tears as he heard the gospel message, perhaps they would ask themselves: *Could my influence allow another human being to end up like Duke?*

I ask people with whom I share a leadership role to abstain from alcohol during the time we work together. My request did not require any of the members of my support team in Phoenix to adjust their lifestyle, except Kayleen.

As a new Christian Kayleen did not share my convictions, and so she asked for leniency in regard to alcohol. When I refused to deviate from my policy, she decided the cause was worth a year of abstinence. After all, she had just delivered a baby and hadn't had a drink for over nine months. How difficult could it be to follow the rule for one year?

For the first few months Kayleen found it difficult to keep her commitment—especially in the areas of criticism, gossip, and maintaining regular devotions. Then her sister came to visit from out of town. During dinner at a restaurant, her sister ordered a glass of wine and encouraged Kayleen to do likewise. In spite of Kayleen's explanation, her sister again urged her to join in the celebration.

"I keenly felt my loss of freedom, but I resisted temptation," Kayleen later said. "That night I was able to refocus my goals and align myself with the purpose of my accountability. Having a drink wasn't that important. More than anything else I wanted to be honest with my accountability partners."

The incident served as a turning point in Kayleen's Christian experience. That didn't surprise me because breaking down a barrier to keep a commitment is good spiritual therapy.

Drug addiction can occur innocently as a result of taking prescription medication. An awareness of potential danger can help us minimize the use of pain killers or other drugs that might become addictive. Anyone who recognizes drug dependency coming on should seek professional help immediately.

In recent years tobacco has been officially classified as a drug. The use of tobacco has long been condemned by many church groups including the one in which I was raised. Christian leaders should also consider the effects of second-hand smoke. If some bars provide a smoke-free environment for the comfort of patrons, surely tobacco use should be taboo at church-related functions.

Workaholics

Confession time.

When Kurt and I lived in Indianapolis, he was the youth minister, and I worked with singles. We worked from fourteen to sixteen hours a day. Through the week people came and left our home as they would any public place, and weekends were tied up with

church events. Our lives were caught up in a whirlwind.

After we had been on that treadmill for about three months, we arrived home from taking a group of singles on a retreat to discover that most of our clothes had relocated from the closet and drawers into the laundry. At four-thirty the following morning we were scheduled to take a youth group to Florida to visit a facility designed to prepare missionaries for the mission field.

As soon as I threw a batch of laundry into the washer, the doorbell rang. While I did laundry, we entertained people from church. Finally, everyone left, and we rushed around to pack for the trip and catch a few hours of sleep.

When we got on the bus the next morning, we had to keep up with an energetic bunch of teens. We had no time for relaxation on the way.

My interest in missions kept me alert as we began to explore the Heart Institute in Florida. We hadn't even finished the tour of the facility when we received two unexpected visitors.

Surprised to see the couple from our church in Indiana, I said, "Audrey! What are you doing here?"

"Gary and I would like to talk to you and Kurt."

Still dazed, I said, "Did you just drive from Indianapolis down here to Florida?"

"That's right."

"How come?"

"Because what we have to say is very important."

Gary and Audrey took us out to a restaurant, and Gary began to talk. "Kurt and Lori," he said, "we have just two words for you. We knew if we told them to you in Indianapolis you wouldn't listen. As we prayed about it we got an impression. So we got in the car and drove seventeen hours to tell you two words."

With our mouths open and our eyes bulging, Kurt and I looked at each other. Gary and Audrey definitely had our attention. I tried to think of something really profound, but I couldn't imagine what they had to say. Finally, I ventured, "What are the two words?"

In a modulated tone of voice, drawing out the words for emphasis, Audrey said, "Slow down."

Kurt blinked. "That's it?"

"Yes."

"You drove seventeen hours to tell us to slow down?"

Gary said, "It's a message from God."

The effort they put forth to deliver the message proved they believed it came from God, but Kurt and I weren't quite sure. "Well, Lori," Kurt said, "why don't we take it to the Lord and get a direct report?"

After Gary and Audrey left, Kurt and I went to our room and got down on our knees. Kurt began to pray. "Lord, we're trying to serve you to the best of our ability. Gary and Audrey brought us two words they say came from you. They tell us to slow down! Is that from you or not?"

From that simple prayer the Spirit of God descended on us, bringing an overwhelming sense of conviction. When Kurt finished praying, we both knew that those two words had traveled from heaven to Indianapolis to be delivered to us in dramatic fashion.

On our own, Kurt and I would have been intimidated at the thought of trying to slow down. We would have reasoned that we had no control of the demands on our time. Convinced that God was directing us, we felt at peace as we began to implement changes in our schedule.

I wish I could say that the incident ended our tendency to overextend ourselves. When work engulfs us, though, we remember a powerful message composed of two words. At those times we allow Jesus to speak to us as he did to the disciples: "Come with me … to a quiet place and get some rest" (Mark 6:31, NIV).

In my work, speaking engagements are scheduled months in advance. If I get a call in January to speak somewhere in June, I look at my blank calendar and say to myself, "No problem." As time goes on, I may receive other invitations I can't turn down. With last-minute obligations and the demands of daily living, my schedule may be packed by June. I haven't yet learned the secret of long-range planning, but I'm working to correct this area of my life.

Reader Challenge

• As you read this chapter did the Holy Spirit remind you of a behavior pattern that needs to be changed? To guide your thinking ask yourself the following questions:

√ *Is my language a good advertisement for God?* Ask a close friend to monitor your conversation to look for expressions that should be eliminated from your speech. Although correct grammar usage is not crucial to your Christian witness, it does enhance your effectiveness in ministry. If people concentrate on grammatical errors, they might miss the message God wants you to convey.

√ *Do my words always represent truth?* Through role-play with a friend, illustrate how you can truthfully answer sensitive questions without hurting the feelings of others. You can learn the art of diplomacy.

√ *Does food have more control over my life than it should?* If you need to make drastic changes in this area, you may want to seek professional help. For minor corrections or to maintain ideal weight, begin a program of discipline. When eating at home, take adequate portions of food but do not go back for seconds. Reduce consumption of foods with high fat or calorie content. Eliminate between-meal snacks. If served snacks at a social function, limit your portion and do not take seconds. Once you establish good

eating habits, you will lose the craving to overindulge your appetite.

√ *Am I building up to a problem with drugs or alcohol?* Even if you have never felt conviction by the Holy Spirit in regard to social drinking, you might want to reevaluate your position in light of the influence you have on others. Remember: what you can do in moderation, others may do in excess. You also need to be aware of the possibility that you might develop dependency on alcohol during times of stress. Check with your doctor on the side effects of prescribed drugs and interaction with any other drugs you are taking.

√ *Have I allowed my work to take control of my life?* To be effective in ministry you need a holy zeal to build God's kingdom. That means you will find more and more to do in order to achieve results. Problems set in when your body will no longer keep pace with your ambitions. What will happen to your ministry if you break down physically or emotionally? In order to do your best for God tomorrow you may need to rest today.

√ *Do I engage in any other destructive behaviors?* A critical spirit or a negative attitude can rob you of the joy that comes from Christian service. An obsession to shop or watch TV (even if you watch good programs) can hinder your effectiveness in ministry. Excesses in any area of your life will reduce the contribution you can make to your Father's business.

• If you have tried repeatedly to break a habit without success, keep on trying. With help from the Holy Spirit some day you will discover the secret formula. For example, say you like clothes but have a weight problem. Declare any additions to your wardrobe off-limits until you build up a fund designated for that purpose. Every time you lose a pound put a specified amount of money in the fund. When you reach your desired weight, go on a shopping spree and have fun.

• Write out what steps you will take to correct any tendency you have toward unbecoming behaviors.

• Adjust the following prayer to your circumstances:

DEAR LORD, thank you for the privilege of serving you. As I endeavor to make the best use of my interests and ability, help me to eliminate anything from my life that would reduce my long-term productivity. God, I feel my task is so enormous that I want to take advantage of every opportunity that comes my way. May I not get caught up in the mechanics of ministry to the point that I fail to rest in you. In Jesus' name I pray. Amen.

1. C. S. Lovett, *Help, Lord, the Devil Wants Me Fat* (Baldwin Park, California: Personal Christianity, 1986).
2. Salierno, 106–108.

CHAPTER 9

The Lure of the Golden Brick

With only a marching band Israel captured Jericho in dramatic fashion, proving that an alliance with God is greater than military might (Josh 6). After that stunning victory, however, God's chosen people suffered defeat in their attempt to take the city of Ai (Josh 7). What made the difference between the two battles? Simply this: Sin had entered the camp.

According to divine instruction, the Israelites had burned the city of Jericho and all the contents except the precious metals and other valuables. This booty they put into the treasury of the house of the Lord. Only one man failed to follow directions. The lure of a golden brick was too much for Achan. He buried the confiscated treasure, hoping to dig it up at an opportune time in the future.

God called Achan to accountability. The entire nation shared in the penalty, but Achan paid the ultimate price with his life and the lives of all members of his family. Greed caused him to lose everything. Achan's death served as a warning to anyone who might be tempted to sacrifice a right relationship with God for material gain.

In the New Testament the Apostle Paul repeatedly warned against greed. He wrote to Timothy, "Those who want to be rich fall into temptation and are trapped by many senseless and harmful desires that plunge people into ruin and destruction. For the love of money is a root of all kinds of evil, and in their eagerness to be rich some have wandered away from the faith" (1 Tim 6:9–10).

Unfortunately, many of those who wander away are leaders in high places. They don't usually move from the faith in one giant leap. Through a series of small steps a church treasurer who borrows cash may end up as an embezzler. A popular television evangelist may collect excess funds from an appeal for support of a particular cause. Eventually, money donated for a missionary effort may end up in the evangelist's pocket.

It's possible, of course, to pursue riches to the detriment of the soul without engaging in fraud. However, even wealth accumulated by truly honorable means displeases God if we place a higher priority on our possessions than on our spiritual experience. In a society where self-worth is measured in terms of material assets, we need to guard against the temptation to accept the world's value system.

Dependence on God

The greater our wealth, the less we seem to depend on God. God wants to participate in every area of our lives—including physical necessities. Jesus told us to pray for our daily bread. We may not often need to take that literally, but if we had to pray down every meal, we would certainly develop a closer relationship with God.

I'm thrilled when I hear testimonies of people who depend on God to meet material needs for extended periods of time. God's ability to come through with the exact amount of money (even to the penny) required to cover bills never ceases to amaze me.

While I was growing up, my family did not experience extreme financial problems. Still, I remember one incident when I was quite small that continues to have an impact on my faith. Dad brought the family together and said, "We don't have enough money for all our bills this month, and so here's what we're going to do. We're going to give our tithe to the church first and trust God to provide enough money for our light bill."

I turned to Mom. "How long will we be living in the dark?"

"Well, until we can get the money," she replied. We then prayed together that God would provide for our needs. Money came through before our lights were turned off.

Another experience after I grew up is even more meaningful. Kurt Salierno and I began to date while we both attended college, and Kurt was spending considerable time ministering to the homeless on skid row in Portland, Oregon. Especially after we became engaged, I had a hard time when Kurt left school to live with the men on the streets. I often walked with him part way.

One evening I was particularly troubled. "Kurt," I said as we neared the place where I would turn around and head back to school, "how are you going to eat while you're there?"

"I don't know, but the Lord has always taken care of me."

My mind recognized truth, but my heart needed reassurance. "I'd feel a lot better if I knew you would eat okay," I said.

Only a few seconds later, a crumpled piece of green paper lying in the gutter caught Kurt's attention. He reached down, picked up a dollar bill, straightened it out, and said, "This is how God is going to feed me."

I stared with wonder at yet another demonstration of God's faithfulness. "Thank you, Lord," my heart repeated all the way back to my dorm.[1]

During mission trips to third world countries, I have seen more evidence of divine providence. When a woman in our group became ill, the rest of us laid hands on her and prayed. Instantly she was healed.

On occasion I've been with groups who were lost in a strange land without a map. After we prayed, directions became as clear as if we were guided by a cloud by day or a pillar of fire by night (see Exodus 13:21–22). Prayer is more effective when we are more dependent upon God.

Financial Planning

My philosophy of money can be simply stated. I believe it's important to decide what lifestyle we want to attain. When we reach the desired economic level, I believe in giving away excess funds to further the kingdom of God.

It becomes a bit tricky when we try to put the philosophy into practice. How do we define our lifestyle?

To a large extent, the house we choose establishes the pace for our standard of living. If we set our sights too high, our goal will require energy and resources that should be spent on service to God.

On the other hand we might aspire to own a house larger than necessary for the purpose of ministry. Especially if we work with small groups, we might want a large room that we reserve for meetings.

When Kurt and I bought a house in Phoenix, we wanted a pool—not for ourselves. I don't even enjoy swimming, but the youth Kurt worked with loved it. Many opportunities to minister to their spiritual needs came during those recreational periods.

Since moving to Georgia, Kurt and I live in a larger house than we need for the two of us. People come and go from our house all the time. We have church functions and dinners, and people often come to spend the night. Since our house payments don't strap us financially, we feel comfortable with the bigger house.

At the same time we recognize God as our ultimate real estate agent. Kurt often says, "If we feel called to meet a need that we can't handle because of house payments, we'll just sell our house, get a smaller one, and meet that need." Sometimes I get nervous when Kurt talks that way because I know such sacrifice would not be easy. Still, I believe our commitment goes deep enough to follow the Lord's leading even if it should take a radical turn.

In defining a lifestyle, we also need to recognize that we may live beyond our wage-earning years. Unless we include plans for retirement, we will eventually come up short. Therefore, we need to build an investment program into the lifestyle we pursue. We must also take inflation into account when we don't know the rate of rising prices twenty or thirty years in the future. Unknown factors complicate a simple philosophy.

As Kurt and I plan for retirement, we are allocating money for travel to different countries to minister to missionaries. I'd like to make a difference on the mission field with encouragement, physical

labor, and financial support. That's my ambition more than Kurt's, but he has comparable ministerial goals that will require money.

At retirement, we will experience a total switch in cash flow. Instead of getting paid to do ministry, we will need to pay out money to do ministry. If we want to realize our dreams for the future, we need to include such provisions in our present budget.

Somewhere along the line we must decide what will happen to our assets when we are gone. Do we want to leave our money to heirs or to the church?

Since Kurt and I don't have children, we don't have a conflict. Some people who have children in ministry may wisely conclude that their money will do the most good for God in the hands of their children.

It's possible to strike a balance between providing for heirs and supporting ministry. One woman set up a trust allocating a specified amount to go to her son upon her death. The balance of funds goes into a charitable remainder trust with a lifetime income to heirs.

Financial planning is not an exact science like accounting, where two and two always equals four. There are enough variables to offset the value of any well-devised program. Seemingly sound investments may fail, we may lose our health, or a natural disaster may destroy our property. Since we cannot possibly guard against all contingencies, we can attain peace of mind only as we place our future in God's hands.

In order to make the best possible decisions regarding financial matters, we will want to seek constant guidance from the Holy Spirit. Our accountability partners can be of tremendous help as they advise us and pray with us regarding this area.

Guarding against Materialism

The reason for setting an upper limit on accumulation of wealth is to avoid idolatry in the form of materialism. Unfortunately, there isn't a magic number that tells us when we have entered the danger zone. We have to make a subjective judgment based on the condition of our heart.

One time a lady came to me and said, "Lori, I have enough money to buy a Mercedes. Do you think I would be happy if I bought a Mercedes?"

I said, "Do you think you might be unhappy with that kind of car?"

"Maybe."

"Why?" I could think of several reasons to be happy with a Mercedes but none to be unhappy.

"I don't know. It's an expensive car."

"Look at your total financial picture. Are you being a good steward of the rest of your money?" I knew her pattern of giving to the church and missions went far beyond the ten percent minimum. "I don't think the car would be a problem," I said. "The problem comes when it grabs your heart."

The cost of the car or anything else is less important than how much we need it to feel good. The psalmist wrote, "If riches increase, do not set your heart on them" (Ps 62:10). We can be wealthy without being materialistic. At the same time we can be materialistic while living in poverty if our main purpose in life is to make money.

For Christmas one year Kurt bought me a sports car. It was a cute little car but much less expensive than a Mercedes. As I started zipping around in my car, people began to notice me. At my health club or in the malls I commanded the kind of attention I liked. One day I pulled up to a stoplight with the top down. A man in the car next to me rolled down his window and said, "That is one nice looking car you have there."

"Thank you very much," I replied. My self-image began to swell, and I started thinking of myself "more highly than [I] ought to think" (Rom 12:3).

Kurt quickly caught on to what was happening to me. "Lori, you're getting a little showy with that car," he said.

When I realized my car was tugging at my heartstrings, I decided it was time to make the matter a subject of prayer. After a brief time of struggle, I prayed, "Lord, if you want me to give up my car, I will."

Shortly after I made that commitment, I felt it would be advisable to continue with my education. When Kurt and I talked about how to finance the project, I said, "I could sell my car."

Kurt's facial expression asked the question even before he said the words. "Are you willing to do that?"

"Yes, because I've just gone through a period of self-examination. God has shown me that maybe my car has too great a pull on my heart."

So far we haven't had to do that, but I still consider it as an option. I want to make sure that I hold any possessions loosely in my hands. Nothing is mine. Everything I have belongs to God and is merely on loan to me. The main thing is to keep focused on the kingdom of heaven and use all my resources for God's glory.

In the area of financial management there are few absolute rules that everyone must follow. Each person needs to develop a personal conviction and live accordingly. That isn't always easy. I'm constantly grappling with questions. Sometimes I almost feel guilty for spending so much money going to third world countries. *Would I be ahead sending the money to missions?* I ask myself. The right answer for me to that question might be different than someone else's answer.

While our accountability partners can't always answer our questions, they can pray with us and help us investigate our motives. When the attitude of our heart is right, we can know we are resting in God's favor.

A good Scripture to guide us regarding materialism comes from the Sermon on the Mount.

Jesus said, "Do not store up for yourselves treasures on earth, where moth and rust consume and where thieves break in and steal; but store up for yourselves treasures in heaven, where neither moth nor rust consumes and where thieves do not break in and steal. For where your treasure is, there your heart will be also" (Matt 6:19–21).

Balancing Faith and Responsibility

Perhaps past generations placed more emphasis on faith than we do today. In many instances God honored faith based on a literal interpretation on the King James Version of Matthew 6:34: "Take therefore no thought for the morrow."

A Bible professor used this verse to make a point about the value of later, more accurate translations of the original Scriptures. In the beginning of the course the professor told his students, "If you take this advice literally, and follow it, you will flunk the course."[2]

Later versions advise against worry about the unknown. There is quite a difference between thinking or planning for tomorrow and worrying about tomorrow. I consider it our responsibility to take steps to ensure financial security for the future. When we have done our best, then faith takes over in trusting God to take care of that over which we have no control.

Of course, we have to be careful we don't go outside God's will in our quest for security. If an attractive job offer that promises to ease a financial crunch would take us out of ministry, faith will need to take precedence over responsibility. In that case we can claim God's promise, "Strive first for the kingdom of God and his righteousness, and all these things will be given to you as well" (Matt 6:33).

Sometimes the Holy Spirit prompts us to leap forward on faith. My greatest faith adventure happened shortly after I aspired to travel to Estonia. "We can't finance the trip from our budget," my practical husband, Kurt, said. "If you go, the money has to fall from the sky."

With the hundred dollars I had on hand I went to the bank. "I want to open a separate account," I told the teller.

As she began to draw up the paperwork, confidence surged through my soul. "I want to tell you why I'm opening this account, and I want you to watch something."

"All right. Why are you opening this account?" the teller said condescendingly.

"In a short time I need twenty-three hundred dollars for a trip to the former Soviet Union, where I'll speak in public schools. I want you to watch with me as God brings this in."

"Whatever." Her tone of voice told me she didn't expect a dramatic build up of my account any time soon.

When I told Kurt, he said, "Lori, don't set yourself up. God sometimes works that way, but it doesn't always happen."

"This time it will."

The following Monday I added eight hundred dollars to the account—an unsolicited donation. I was excited, but Kurt reminded me I still had a long way to go.

Two Sundays later a lady came up to me at church and said, "Lori, I don't know why, but I think God wants me to give you a thousand dollars."

"That's too much money from one person," I said to the older woman. I hoped she would offer me part of that amount, but she didn't.

When I told Kurt, he said, "You're really testing your faith, aren't you? After making a radical claim to the bank, you refuse the thousand dollars God puts in your hands. You amaze me!"

I could see his point. but I couldn't very well go back and tell the woman I'd changed my mind. All I could do was pray, "God, if you want me to have that money, then have her come back to me. Otherwise, I'm not going to worry about it."

A few weeks later, the woman said, "Lori, I can't get over the feeling that I need to give you a thousand dollars. You're just going to have to take it because I can't get any peace until you do." Perhaps she wondered why I needed no further coaxing.

My next deposit impressed the bank teller. She continued to be astonished as I brought in the rest of the money, collected in similar fashion.

Some of my attempts to finance a project on faith have met with failure rather than success. Fortunately,

I had not told anyone outside the church to watch what God would do. A claim that doesn't come true raises questions about the validity of faith. For our witness to be effective, we need to keep faith and responsibility in perspective.

As we endeavor to maintain a proper balance between faith and responsibility, our accountability partners can once again be of assistance. Through prayer, Scripture, and sound advice we can find a balance that gives us peace of mind.

Sacrificial Giving

When David wanted to erect an altar to the Lord on a certain threshing floor, the owner offered to give David the property along with oxen for the burnt offering. David replied, "No, but I will buy them from you for a price; I will not offer burnt offerings to the Lord my God that cost me nothing" (2 Sam 24:24).

Some people think they can get away with giving God something they don't want anyway. For our giving to bring glory to God and spiritual benefit to us, it needs to represent a piece of our heart. By our sacrifice, we show we love God more than any treasure we hold dear.

Before my first trip to India, I didn't go to the mall for a year and a half. That might not be a great sacrifice for some people, but it was for me. In order to go on the trip I had to save money I ordinarily spent on clothes.

Now, more than ten years later, I'm still feasting on spiritual manna I received during that trip. The clothes I might have bought would be outdated, worn out, or both.

Several people made tremendous sacrifices in order to go with me on my second trip to India. People thought of creative ways to raise money. Some worked second jobs. A college student even sold her car, which she would be unable to replace in the foreseeable future. Because of the sacrifice involved, we had an incredible trip. Giving from the heart made God's blessings more meaningful.

So far I haven't had to figure out how to sacrifice out of an affluent lifestyle, but some people do. With a strong enough balance sheet they can make a sizeable contribution to God's kingdom without feeling much pain.

It's important for people of means to discover a way to obtain the kind of joy that comes from both planning and real sacrifice. One woman I know about opened a separate bank account into which she deposits the same amount each month. Clothes and certain other expenditures must come from that account. When she sees a need that goes beyond her regular giving, the woman sometimes gives up the new outfit or other item she planned to purchase in order to meet the need.

"Maybe it's pseudo-sacrifice," she says, "because I'm not down to my last dollar. In any event, the discipline is of value."

Time is a precious commodity to many people. For these people, giving a few hours to lift the quality of life for someone else constitutes sacrifice. That might mean taking an elderly person to the doctor, listening to someone pour out a tale of sorrow, or praying with someone regarding a spiritual need. It might mean providing a place to stay for a missionary on furlough or just being available to someone in a crisis.

Many of Satan's ploys to cause us to stumble center around money. Our adversary, the devil, tells us we can't depend on God and that a sense of security comes from ever-increasing wealth and possessions. He tries to use our possessions as a wedge between us and our devotion to God.

The bottom line of a balance sheet reveals the monetary strength of a company or an individual. For Christians the spiritual bottom line is the condition of the heart. If we use all that we have and all that we are for the kingdom of God, the numbers on our financial statement won't really matter.

Reader Challenge

- Write out your philosophy of money.
- What kind of lifestyle do you hope to attain ten years from now? Project your goals for retirement. Develop a financial plan that will enable you to realize your goals. How do you need to adjust your

present lifestyle to include funds for long-range plans?

• List all of your assets and possessions. Which ones are you willing to dedicate to God's use? Do any of them tug at your heartstrings? Will you ask for power from the Holy Spirit to relinquish everything you have to God?

• Write out how you will balance faith and responsibility.

• How will you give God a sacrificial offering in the coming week?

• In spiritual terms what is the bottom line of your financial statement?

• Would your stewardship prayer resemble the one below?

GOD, thank you for allowing me to enjoy many of the good things you have created. Thank you for the ability to earn money and for the privilege of investing it back into your kingdom. As I now dedicate everything I have and everything I am to you, may I never shift my focus from you to the things of the world. When I forget, remind me that you have promised to "fully satisfy every need of [mine] according to [your] riches in glory in Christ Jesus. To ... God ... be glory forever and ever. Amen" (Phil 4:19–20).

1. Salierno, 33–34.
2. George H. Ramsey, Sr., *Tools for Bible Study* (Anderson, Indiana: Warner Press, 1971), 34.

CHAPTER 10

Accountability at the Crossroads

By his response, David sentenced himself to death. The king took literally the prophet's story about a rich man who stole a poor man's only lamb. "[David] said to Nathan, 'As the Lord lives, the man who has done this deserves to die; he shall restore the lamb fourfold, because he did this thing, and because he had no pity' " (2 Sam 12:5–6).

I imagine Nathan remained silent for a moment, allowing the king's anger to burn against the culprit. Then, with authority ringing in his voice, he declared, "You are the man!" (v 7).

Stunned, David listened as Nathan explained the parable. He had to recognize himself as the rich man who took Bathsheba from Uriah, the poor man. After stealing Uriah's wife, David tried to cover up his deed with murder! The crime of stealing a sheep paled in comparison.

At that point the king had to make a decision. Would he confess and repent or would he sink deeper

into sin? According to the law, a prophet who delivered a message not commanded by God should be put to death (Deut 18:20). As king, David need only issue the order to forever silence his accuser.

Standing at the crossroads, David decided to settle his account with God. Because he chose the path of righteousness, David is remembered as a man after God's heart (Acts 13:22).

The Wrong Turn

If we look for biblical examples of leaders who came to a crossroads and turned the wrong way, we find many. After division of the Jewish nation, all of the kings of Israel and most of the kings of Judah chose to lead the people away from God and into idolatry.

In the New Testament, Judas, of course, stands out as the prime example of the leader who made a dramatic departure from righteousness. As one of the disciples personally chosen by Jesus to carry on the work of the kingdom, Judas allied himself with the enemy. Driven by greed, the man who served as the first church treasurer sold his Master for thirty pieces of silver. He then sealed his bargain with a fatal kiss.

The remorse that Judas felt after Jesus was condemned to die did not cause him to seek reconciliation with the Savior. He tried to rid himself of guilt by returning the money he once coveted. Hurling down the coins in the temple, Judas went out and hanged himself (Matt 27:3–10).

While the actions of Judas will always horrify us, current examples of fallen leaders are no less damaging to the kingdom of God. The whole world quickly learns about prominent pastors or leaders who decide to ignore the right way. Through their sins, they are crucifying again the Son of God and are holding him up to contempt (Heb 6:6).

A comment made during an annual ministerial assembly representing an entire church movement continues to haunt me. At the beginning of the meeting the leader said, "This year we meet with fewer people because some of our members have made some unwise choices."

Through my work with Christian colleges I sometimes observe faculty members or students standing at the crossroads. All too often they take the wrong turn.

At the close of one of my sessions I felt the need to establish a leadership base for the students. "I'd like to address the faculty members," I said. "Will those of you who will commit to be Christian role models for the students please come forward?" Several people came, and we had prayer together. The public act of consecration benefited faculty members and students alike.

Turning on Faith

When God signals us to turn, we have no guarantee that the path will be smooth. We are required to travel on faith, not knowing where the journey will lead.

While on a pleasant road, my friend Gwen began to question whether or not she was going in the right direction. She was dating a man I'll call Walter (not his real name). Walter had a lot to offer in looks, personality, and financial security, but he demonstrated little evidence of Christian faith.

Gwen and I went out to lunch one day and she began to talk. "I like everything about Walter," she said, "except I'm not convinced that his walk with God is real."

"Do you know what to do about it?"

Her inner struggle registered on her face. Finally, she spoke, "I think I know what to do, but my heart doesn't want to break up with him."

She had come to the crossroads, and I had to ask a hard question. "If you end up marrying a non-Christian, do you think God will honor that relationship?"

"Well, I don't know."

We talked about people we both knew who had married outside the faith. Some of the stories portrayed a bleak outlook for happiness. Not only were marriages in trouble, Christians had lost their zeal for serving God.

"The decision is yours," I said, after pointing out all the pitfalls. "Your whole future hinges on one fragile moment when you decide whether to follow your heart or your head."

A few weeks later Gwen and I went out to lunch again. Her troubled expression had been replaced by an aura of peace. I listened as she related her conversation with Walter.

On their last date, Gwen had said, "Walter, you're everything I want in a man. You're handsome and have a good job. You're nice and courteous, but you don't love the Lord."

"What difference does that make if I have everything else you want?"

"It makes all the difference in the world to me."

"Don't you think we could solve that issue if I don't object to your going to church?'

"Perhaps we could, but I'm choosing not to."

Walter continued to argue, but Gwen remained true to her convictions. "I really felt strong in the Lord after I made that decision," she said.

With no prospects of anyone else to date, Gwen followed God's prompting. For her, faith found a fast reward. In a matter of months she met a strong Christian man whom she later married, but that isn't always the case. The right decision sometimes carries a high cost.

After rejecting the sexual advances of Potiphar's wife, Joseph spent two years in prison. That was a tough break, but Joseph did not give up on God or become bitter. Eventually Joseph's integrity earned him a position of power in Egypt. Looking back on all the suffering he had endured, Joseph said, "God intended it for good" (Gen 50:20).

Standing at the crossroads, we need to base our decision on the long-term effects. That will cause us to make the right decision regardless of what the short-term consequences may be. As with that old folk song, we will sing, "I have decided to follow Jesus; No turning back, no turning back."

If we experience pain as a result of doing what is right, we know our affliction is only temporary. We can handle present hardship if we set our sights on our eternal reward. In the meantime, God will honor our efforts and help us develop a quality of life unattainable without divine favor.

Racing with Caution

I couldn't talk the policeman out of giving me a ticket. Although I knew I had stretched the limit regarding traffic rules, I wasn't ready to pay the fine without further discussion. Therefore I went before the judge.

Dressed in his official black robe, the solemn judge depicted authority. Underneath his professional demeanor, however, I surmised the distinguished gentleman had a sense of humor. I liked him immediately.

"Mrs. Salierno, you ran a red light."

"Yes, sir."

"Do you plead guilty or not guilty?"

"Guilty, your honor, with an explanation."

Lowering his eyeglasses, he said, "All right. Let me hear your explanation."

"The light turned yellow, and I knew it would turn red in only a few seconds. I figured I could speed up and get through it before it turned red. I just want you to know I didn't intend to break the law. The red light just slipped up on me."

He removed his glasses, and his gaze penetrated my being. "Mrs. Salierno, you can learn something from this. You'll come to a lot of intersections, and you'll always have a decision to make. You know what you should do, and you know what you want to do. You think it won't matter, but those who do what they should do don't end up where you are right now."

At that point I wished I had paid the fine without trying to offer an explanation. The judge was right, and I should have practiced a principle I had learned years before in Sunday school.

"I'd like to do something for you, Mrs. Salierno," the judge continued. "I trust you've learned your lesson, and so I'm not going to make you pay the fine. But I'd like to challenge you. The next time you see a light turn yellow, do what you know is right." His stern expression relaxed, and a hint of merriment danced in his eyes. "Then you won't be here looking at my face, and I won't be looking at yours. That way we'll both be happy."

As I left the court house I took the judge's words with me. That which applies to caution lights applies also to life. The yellow light of God's Word is found in Hebrews 2:1: "We must pay more careful attention, therefore, to what we have heard, so that we do not drift away" (NIV).

It's easy to rationalize that minor infractions of holy living won't matter. Someone who dislikes mundane tasks may excuse a shoddy performance in areas where no one will notice. The gregarious person may reason that no one will get hurt from an innocent flirtation. Some people might consider personal use of time or resources that belong to the boss to be perks of the job.

A flashing yellow light sometimes signals neglect of our devotions. The Holy Spirit reminds us to slow down and spend time with the Lord, but we hurry on our way. Unless we stop at the caution light, we'll miss what God wants to say to us.

U-Turns

As Christian leaders involved in evangelistic efforts, we tell non-Christians they need to turn around and go in the opposite direction. Sometimes, though, we don't want to make such a radical change ourselves.

Zacchaeus made a complete turnabout after a brief encounter with Jesus. Without any prompting Zacchaeus said, "Look, half of my possessions, Lord, I will give to the poor; and if I have defrauded anyone of anything, I will pay back four times as much" (Luke 19:8).

The most dramatic conversion I ever witnessed didn't happen in church. After moving to the Atlanta area, I joined a health club and enrolled in an aerobics class. I'll call the leader Tonya (not her real name).

With her well-built body and congenial personality, Tonya commanded my admiration immediately.

I went up to her after class and introduced myself. "I really appreciate the enthusiastic way you teach," I said.

"Well," she said, "I might have enthusiasm for aerobics, but I don't have enthusiasm for life." The turmoil that churned inside clouded her face. Tonya went on to describe feelings of depression. "I have no direction," she said. "Something is tugging at me. I don't know what it is or what to do about it."

Not often do I find someone so honest and straightforward during an initial meeting. I seized the opportunity to introduce her to Jesus Christ. "I think I might know a Source that can give you direction and get you through depression. It's the same Source that's tugging at you."

Tonya stared at me in disbelief. "Are you for real?"

When I affirmed an offer of real help, Tonya wanted to get together right away. A few days later we met for breakfast.

"Tell me about this Source," she said before we even had a chance to get acquainted.

Never have I had anyone respond so quickly to the gospel presentation. With tears in her eyes, she said, "That's what I need." Tonya had no inhibitions about asking God for the gift of salvation in the small shop where we ate.

By the time I returned from a speaking engagement, the woman, who had been heavy into drinking, had already led her boyfriend and her oldest brother to the Lord. Leaving her old lifestyle behind, Tonya began to make new friends and discover joy in different kinds of activities.

With Zacchaeus and Tonya as examples, do Christian leaders have any excuse for failing to turn around and go in the direction the Lord leads? It isn't always sin that requires us to make a U-turn. We might need to change the focus of our ministry to be more effective in God's kingdom. A person in a secular job might have to give up a good salary to enter full-time ministry with no guarantee of financial security.

As we consider changing directions in matters that do not involve right and wrong, we will want to seek input from our accountability partners. Through prayer and godly counsel, we can discern the leading of the Holy Spirit.

Detours

A trouble area on the highway interrupts our travel. We must take an alternate route until the problem is fixed and we can rejoin the main road. Our journey with the Lord is similar.

Jesus said, "When you are offering your gift at the altar, if you remember that your brother or sister has something against you, leave your gift there before the altar and go; first be reconciled to your brother or sister, and then come and offer your gift" (Matt 5:23–24).

Until our wrongs are rectified, we will have difficulty staying on the right road spiritually. An apology might make amends or restitution might call for a more tangible form of repair.

When I was a freshman in high school I had a hard time with physical education. I liked the athletic part but I disliked undressing in front of the other girls to take a shower.

The instructor assigned each girl a number. She kept a chart showing who took showers.

One day I decided I just couldn't face undressing, taking a shower, and struggling back into my clothes. I skipped the shower. *What difference would it make to anyone whether or not I took a shower?* I reasoned.

My real problem surfaced when the instructor called my number at the end of the session. "Twenty-three took a shower," I said. Even as she checked off my chart, my conscience began to whisper, "You lied!"

By dinner time I was so miserable I just picked at my food. "Lori, is something wrong?" Mom asked.

"Yeah, I did something wrong, I think."

"What did you do?" Dad asked.

I explained what had happened. As I tried to justify my action, Dad interrupted. "If it's not that big a deal and doesn't matter, then why aren't you eating?" he asked.

I had lived with that conflict all day. "Because I told a lie," I said. "Dad, what do you think I should do?"

"I don't think I need to tell you. I think you already know." That was just like Dad to throw the responsibility back to me.

When I confessed to the instructor, she expressed surprise. "Why are you telling me this?"

"Because I told a lie, and I can't live with myself until I make it right."

She told me to run a lap, and we'd forget about it. I distinctly remember the freedom I felt as I ran that lap.

When we come to a crossroads, it doesn't matter whether the issue is of major or minor importance. A principle is at stake even if no one will be affected by our action. Any compromise of principle will bring leanness to the soul. Whether we need to approach the crossroads with caution, turn on faith, make a U-turn, or take a detour, we can make the right move by following wise counsel and the leadership of the Holy Spirit.

Reader Challenge

• How did you handle your last major decision? Your last minor decision? If you made the wrong turn, what can you now do to turn the situation around?

• If you contemplate making a turn on faith, write out the possible consequences, both positive and negative.

√ Positive consequences:

√ Negative consequences:

• What might you miss if you don't step out on faith?

• Identify an area of your life where you need to put up a caution light. What Scripture will you hide in your heart to help you maintain discipline regarding this issue?

• As you pray, listen for God's voice. How might you personalize this prayer?

DEAR GOD, thank you for providing a road map to travel life's highway. When I come to a crossroads, help me to seek direction from your Word. If I need to turn on faith, help me disregard possible pitfalls and concentrate on the joy of remaining in your favor. Help me to take caution lights seriously, make a U-turn if necessary, and take a detour when trouble interrupts my travel. In the name of Jesus I pray. Amen.

CHAPTER 11

Discerning False Signals

Although other people can greatly assist us in hearing from God, we have to choose carefully which voices to heed and which ones to ignore. The Bible instructs us: "Don't always believe everything you hear just because someone says it is a message from God: test it first to see if it really is. For there are many false teachers around" (1 John 4:1, LIVING BIBLE).

Some years ago a man in California started out as an effective pastor adhering to biblical teaching. Little by little his message started to veer off course, but no one challenged him. When his congregation reached nearly a thousand, he said to his followers, "Why don't we all go to Guyana? With no distractions, we can be very focused on God's voice."

In Guyana the pastor's teachings became even more bizarre. One day he passed out little paper cups filled with grape-flavored drink laced with cyanide. He said, "Listen to the voice of God. Drink it."

The mass suicide caught media attention. Reports that followed showed Christians looking ridiculous.

When I was in high school a man in our church taught a Bible study in his home, using certain biblical facts to distort truth. One Bible distortion was based on the life of Jacob. After working seven years to gain Rachel as his bride, Jacob received Leah. In order to marry Rachel, the love of his life, he had to work seven more years. What was the lesson to be learned from that story, according to this home Bible study leader? "God still wants men to have two or three wives."

No one in the group disagreed. No one pointed to 1 Timothy 3:12 that stresses monogamous marriage relationships. Encouraged by the silent reception, he went a step further. The married man with four children said, "God has revealed to me that one of you in this group will soon have a special place in my life."

I had a friend in that Bible study I'll call Michelle (not her real name). Michelle came to me and said, "Lori, this Bible study is richer and deeper than anything we get at church. You ought to come."

"If it's so rich and deep, why don't the people in your Bible study come to church any longer?"

"It's too shallow."

"Michelle," I said, "be very careful of your Bible study leader. Following someone who no longer wants to be accountable to the church can be dangerous!"

The leader of that Bible study urged Michelle to marry him in a spiritual sense. "We won't do it the legal way. People wouldn't understand, but God is telling you to be married to me."

This man's power over my friend was great enough to convince her that wrong was right. She ended up pregnant, and became an emotional, physical, and spiritual wreck from which she never recovered.

A charismatic personality or someone with the gift of communication can lead others to spiritual destruction. To avoid being deceived we need to test each message and the messenger according to biblical guidelines.

The Jesus Test

The Scripture that tells us to check out the authenticity of those who claim to share God's Word also gives us a criterion for making a judgment. "The way to find out if their message is from the Holy Spirit is to ask: Does it really agree that Jesus Christ, God's Son, actually became man with a human body? If so, then the message is from God" (1 John 4:2, LIVING BIBLE).

Without divinity, Christ would have been no more than a good man and a great teacher. He would not be our advocate with the Father, our intercessor, or our Savior. Through him we could not receive forgiveness of our sins or have hope of eternal life. Unless Christ is fully human and fully divine the church might as well go out of business.

Christ is the foundation of our faith and any message must be built on him. Teaching that denies the deity of Christ, the virgin birth, or salvation through the death and resurrection of Jesus does not pass the test.

As the head of the church, Jesus is our role model. Human role models are valuable only as they mirror the image of Christ. Likewise, we can accept signals from others only if they conform to the life and teachings of Jesus. When someone suggests we take a certain action, we should ask ourselves, *Would it make me more like Christ?*

How can we discern what will make us more like Christ and what won't? We can compare the suggested action with Christ's actions and biblical teaching.

For instance, suppose someone were to propose hiring a professional to perform acrobatic stunts on the roof of the church to attract attention. Should the suggestion be made a matter of prayer or brought to the church for a vote? Not if we remember how Jesus reacted to the temptation to jump from the pinnacle of the temple (Luke 4:9–12).

Jesus based his conduct on Scripture. Only the Old Testament was written at the time, but we also have benefit of the divinely inspired writings of the apostles. If we want to confirm our judgment concerning the acrobat, we can turn to 1 Corinthians 14:40: "All things should be done decently and in order."

The more familiar we become with God's Word, the better able we will be to discern false signals. Some situations call for quick decisions. Only Scripture committed to memory can help us at that point. God speaks to us through a verse that pops into our minds at an opportune moment.

New Revelations

I always get leery when someone claims to have a new revelation from God. Never before revealed truth often contradicts truth already revealed. In times of personal reflection we can receive fresh insights into old truths, but "there is no variation or shadow due to change" (James 1:17) regarding God. "I the Lord do not change" (Mal 3:6).

New ideas or impressions can be tested through the church family. After taking the gospel to the Gentiles, the Apostle Paul wrote, "[God's] intent was that now, through the church, the manifold wisdom of God should be made known" (Eph 3:10, NIV). People who break fellowship with a true family of believers over an issue usually end up outside the Lord's will because God works through the church.

As suspicious as I am of anyone professing to have a new revelation, I'm even more skeptical of people who claim to have a revelation for me. I always wonder, *Why me? Why don't they get their own word from God?*

A man called me up one time and said, "Lori, I have a word from God for you."

His words didn't surprise me. I frequently hear similar comments. "Okay, I'm listening," I said.

"This is too important to tell you over the phone. I want to make an appointment."

Some time later the man sat down with me and said, "Lori, this word is specific concerning your life, and I want you to hear it and obey."

To this older gentleman I said, "Sir, may I ask you something before you tell me the word from God?"

"Yes."

"I want you to know that I spend time with God every day. God already has an avenue to communicate with me. I will listen to anything you have to say to me, but I ask you to give me the freedom to discern whether or not that word came from God. Will you give me that?"

He thought a moment, and then he said, "Yes. Here's the word of God for you. In the next six weeks you will be pregnant, you will go off the speaking circuit, and you will move to the northwest."

Years later, I'm still waiting to get pregnant, opportunities on the road are opening up even more, and here I am living in Georgia. The man struck out three times.

I don't mean to imply that God never sends us a message through others. On occasion I have received an authentic word from God through other people. In most instances the message confirmed what I had already heard from God. After my own encounters with God, questions often remain. *Did I hear the Lord*

rightly? Shall I move ahead on my impression? A confirmation from someone else helps remove the questions.

Satan's Signals

When it comes to sending false signals, Satan operates at his best. It seems incredible that the devil could put thoughts in our heads and make us believe they came from God, but Scripture confirms this is true: "Satan disguises himself as an angel of light" (2 Cor 11:14). In fact, the evil one often works when we least expect it.

For instance, while the program of a local congregation works smoothly, Satan plants a note of discord into someone's heart. A few others agree. Soon opposing factions begin to operate. Each side may have merit, but the devil is the real winner. He has diverted the mission of the church from saving souls to debating a petty issue.

Satan can even convince us to do something good for immature reasons. Suppose a thought comes to us, *If I bake cookies and take them to the residents of a nursing home, everyone will see how wonderful I am.* Is that God speaking? Certainly, the thought of baking cookies for the elderly is a godly suggestion. Even motivation based on getting a pat on the head from persons important to us is fairly normal for us when we are youngsters. However, by the time we are adults, actions should be prompted by higher motivations than public acclaim.

In the school of demonology, Satan took his graduate work in human psychology. He knows how to convince a demented mind to kill someone and claim the command came from God. At the same time he can induce Christians to deviate from demonstrating the fruit of the spirit.

When God's Voice Is Vetoed

The experience is common to most Christian leaders. At one time or another we believe we know the mind of God but circumstances or someone blocks our mission. We feel called to serve on a church board, but we lose out in the election. Or, no one else will support the cause God put on our heart.

What to do? If the vote seems to veto the voice of God, maybe we confused our own ambition with God's voice. Even if God did call us to serve, we are not responsible for a closed door. We are only required to be willing to serve when God provides an opportunity. While waiting for a door to open we can use the time to good advantage. Perhaps more Bible study or training in human relations will better prepare us for service.

If others fail to endorse a cause we hold dear, we could continue the campaign to change minds. "God told me to do it this way," we might say. The argument sounds persuasive, but it will likely turn others off. Who wants to be placed in the position of having to argue with God? Our crusade will be more effective if we take our hands off and allow God to handle it at the right time.

In the following example of a pastor who expected his congregation to accept his personal interpretation of God's will, some of the details as well as the names have been changed to protect individual privacy.

When Pastor Blake went to First Church he dreamed of reaching the masses for Christ. With a congregation of over one hundred strong members, he envisioned them doing great things together. Of course, they would need a larger facility to handle the new people. Before winning even one convert to the Lord, Pastor Blake started pushing for a new sanctuary.

"We just finished our fellowship hall," the chairman of the board said. "The people aren't ready for another building program yet. Besides, our present sanctuary is more than adequate."

"It won't be when we pull in people from this new housing development going up. They aren't going to come if we don't have a place to put them."

Members of the board discussed the matter and decided the pastor's reasoning was sound but concluded he was trying to move too quickly.

"When people start coming, we can extend our present sanctuary out back," the pastor was told.

"But God is telling me to move ahead now. Where is your faith? Are you going to hinder God's program?" the pastor argued back.

Almost every sermon Pastor Blake preached promoted his agenda. People started leaving the church. The pastor regarded them as troublemakers and did not mourn their departure. More people left the church until finally, Pastor Blake was forced to resign. Not only did the pastor's dream come to naught, the congregation was weakened in the process.

When God gives us a vision, we may have to overcome many obstacles before we reach our goal. A signal from God doesn't require overnight accomplishment. With patience and prayer we can survive opposition and might even bring some of the dissident members onto the team.

"Lord, bring us together in unity. Permeate our minds with the same message according to your will," is a good way to pray. As we voice public prayer, a humble spirit indicating an openness to divine direction will encourage others to do likewise. The value of building a consensus will offset any missed opportunities caused by delay.

Deviation from Divine Authority

In my entire ministry the signal that caused me the greatest confusion came from a role model and close friend—a godly person who had given me sound advice on several previous occasions. I'll call her Miss Wesley.

Shortly after I became engaged to Kurt Salierno, Miss Wesley came to me and said, "I want to encourage you to break off your engagement."

Shocked, I asked, "Why?"

She gave me the standard argument about a sea full of fish. *But I don't want a fish, I want a husband, I was thinking.*

Then she voiced her real concern. "He will hinder your ministry." While she didn't exactly outline my present speaking career, she projected a similar future.

Because of Miss Wesley's professional standing and the confidence I had built up in her, I overruled my own judgment and broke up with Kurt.

Infuriated, Kurt confronted the woman. "How dare you interfere in my life?" he demanded. "Who gave you the authority to play God?"

Miss Wesley called me. "Why did you tell Kurt what I said?"

"You told me to break up with him, and I did. He wanted to know why, and I thought he deserved to hear the truth."

This lady who had been like a mother to me for two years said, "Let me tell you something. We have to have space in our relationship now because I've overstepped my bounds, and it's not working out. So I'm going to have to distance myself from you."

In spite of my protests, Miss Wesley insisted we must take separate paths. I was devastated but, fortunately, Kurt and I got back together. On my wedding day she called to congratulate me. Her courteous but distant manner indicated she still thought I was making a mistake.

A few years later Kurt and I were working in a church not far from where Miss Wesley had moved. A few months after she started coming to our church, Miss Wesley called Kurt and me to her home.

Kurt and I were both nervous, but she quickly put us at ease. "I've watched you two work together and, Lori, I want you to know I was wrong in asking you not to get married. I've never been married myself, and I've only seen men hinder women in their ministry. Kurt, you're one exceptional man, and I love you."

Even the best among us can be mistaken in assessing what someone else should do. The Apostle Paul's "wish that all were as I myself am [unmarried]" (1 Cor 7:7) would not be right for everyone. Paul later indicated that his suggestion came from himself and not from God.

We need to weigh carefully even the counsel we receive from people living close to God. Because personal experience can so easily color our judgment, we also need to take a cautious approach when advising others.

When someone disagrees with me, I always think back to Miss Wesley. What if I had not disagreed with her? I've told students they need to go to a certain school, but they have chosen to go against my advice. As it turns out occasionally, they have been right and I have been wrong.

The possibility of failing to discern a false signal is scary. If we keep open hearts, pray for direction,

and make deliberate decisions, we can walk forward with confidence.

Reader Challenge

• As you read this chapter, did you recall a time when you thought you had a word from God but later learned you were wrong? How did you discover the source of your signal? What did you learn from the experience?

• If you are serving God and making a difference in the kingdom of heaven, Satan is sure to send you signals. How do you recognize Satan's signals, and what do you do about them?

• Imagine yourself in Pastor Blake's situation. When would you have changed your course of action, and what would you have done?

• In your teaching and counseling, are you careful to differentiate between biblical standards and your personal convictions? Christians are required to live up to God's standards as revealed in Scripture, but they are not bound by your personal interpretation of what is best for them.

• What can you do now to help you discern false signals in the future? Cultivate a Christlike characteristic? Saturate your mind with Scripture so you will recognize false teaching? Find a place in a small Christian community where you can share your doubts and receive guidance? Will you set a goal and make a commitment to carry out one step toward that goal?

• Make your commitment with a prayer:

HEAVENLY FATHER, thank you for your willingness to converse with me. Help me to hear your voice eagerly, and protect me from other voices that would lead me astray. Through your Word and the example of Jesus I promise to draw closer to you so that I can discern your voice from that of a stranger. In Jesus' name I pray. Amen.

CHAPTER 12

Restoring Fallen Leaders

At this point we shift our focus from prevention to therapy. In spite of provisions to the contrary, Christian leaders sometimes succumb to sin. No one is immune to the possibility. The Bible warns us: "So if you think you are standing, watch out that you do not fall" (1 Cor 10:12).

The question then becomes: How do we handle leaders who yield to temptation either unintentionally or deliberately? If the leader is a high-profile individual, we can be sure the secular media will rush in for the kill. Those unsympathetic to the Christian community enjoy disclosing a religious leader's fall from grace.

Unfortunately, no leader falls without adversely affecting others. Unbelievers quickly grab an excuse to continue to reject Christ. "I'm not as bad as the preacher," they say. Weak Christians often become discouraged to the point of giving up when a leader they greatly admire falls.

Sin that has been exposed in someone holding a high ranking position in the church causes embarrassment for other leaders. The man who replaces a treasurer found guilty of embezzlement will wonder if congregational members question his integrity. If a woman caught in adultery happens to be a Sunday school teacher, the actions of every Sunday school teacher will be scrutinized more carefully. Maintaining Christian conduct while others expect failure is painful.

The transgression of one minister can hinder the effectiveness of another. For instance, a message on holiness might be met with skepticism if a ministerial colleague with a pious demeanor has been convicted of sexually molesting a child.

Perhaps because the repercussions for misconduct of Christian leaders are so severe, we might be tempted to judge the offenders harshly—as though they are beyond redemption. We tend to resent the adverse reflection their indiscretions place on our lives and ministry. It would be easy to wish they would just go away, but what does the Bible say?

Gently Restore

"My friends, if anyone is detected in a transgression, you who have received the Spirit should restore such a one in a spirit of gentleness" (Gal 6:1). That sounds like clear-cut instruction, but how does it apply to real life?

When I worked with singles in Indianapolis, I saw leadership potential in several members of the group and wanted to help them develop their ability. For that purpose I set up a leadership council. Meeting for two hours each week, we spent the first hour functioning as a task-oriented group to define goals and carry them out. We devoted the second hour to accountability.

To help us become effective in our mission, we all signed a covenant agreement, binding for one year. We pledged to love each other and witness for Christ, as well as to maintain personal spiritual disciplines consisting of prayer, Bible study, and Scripture memorization.

In keeping with the call for holy living, we promised to abstain from alcohol, drugs, or tobacco. To maintain sexual purity, we vowed to control our thoughts and avoid seductive literature or movies.

At first everyone cooperated enthusiastically. Members of the group couldn't wait to share high points in their spiritual life. For the first few weeks, the mood of the meetings was definitely upbeat.

Two or three months later, however, a few members of the group started to complain about the demands on their lives. Hard work subdued the thrill of spiritual conquest. Crucifying the flesh began to get painful.

"What are you saying to me?" I asked. "Are you saying you can continue with this, or do you need to get out?" If they would discipline themselves according to our agreement, I promised they would produce a quality in their spiritual lives that's rare in the church today. "With that blessing comes a price," I said. "Are you willing to pay it?" After considering the cost, they all decided to remain on the team.

Even after making that recommitment, a man I'll call Hal (not his real name) violated the covenant. During the business portion of the meeting, he remained quiet and seemed somewhat edgy. As soon as we began to discuss accountability, he spoke up. "With all of you I signed an agreement that I would not drink alcoholic beverages, but I want you to know I got drunk last Friday."

Except for Hal's muffled sobs, the room became extremely quiet, and all eyes focused on me. "Why are you looking at me?" I said. "He covenanted with you, too. "So we as a group are going to deal with it. What do you think?"

"Why did you get drunk?" someone said.

"I don't know. It just happened," he said with anguish ringing in his voice.

"Are you sorry?"

"Yes, I am."

"Are you going to do it again?"

"No, I won't do it again."

Neglecting the admonition to be gentle, one girl said, "Well, if you're sorry and you're not going to do it again, why did you do it in the first place?"

"I don't need judgment. I need healing and forgiveness," Hal pleaded.

After members of the group finished the process of evaluating the situation, the penitent man looked at me and said, "Am I still in the group?"

"Ask them," I said.

Everyone agreed. Because Hal was sincerely sorry and promised to refrain from the use of alcohol, they allowed him to remain in the group. That decision turned out to be right. Surrounded by the redemptive attitude of his peers, Hal began to grow in the Lord. I saw him a few years after I left Indianapolis. Referring to the affirmation he received from members of the accountability group, he said, "That was the turning point in my spiritual life."

Sever Relationship

Another verse from Scripture seemingly contradicts the call for restoration. "Now I am writing to you not to associate with anyone who bears the name of brother or sister who is sexually immoral or greedy, or is an idolater, reviler, drunkard, or robber. Do not even eat with such a one" (1 Cor 5:11).

A few years after the incident with Hal, I was working with a different group under a similar structure. One time a man came to the meeting and confessed he had engaged in an illicit sexual relationship.

The news surprised and grieved everyone. Again I left the decision up to members of the group.

Through tears they discussed their options. Expressing their love and assuring the man of their forgiveness, they asked him to leave the group. They didn't cut him off from the body of Christ, but they did suspend his leadership role.

"Does this mean I'm not useful to God's kingdom?" he asked.

I wasn't sure how to answer, but I said, "When you join yourself to someone in that way, you need a period of healing. You need to reestablish your relationship with the Lord. In time you'll be ready for leadership again."

At the time I felt the decision was right, and I still do, but sometimes I have misgivings. During one of my visits to Indianapolis, the man and I were at the same party. I brought up the subject of accountability and asked, "How did you feel about being asked to leave the group?"

"It was very painful, and I'm not sure I agreed with it—as if all of you were perfect. But I'm not holding it against you."

I'm grateful the man has remained in the church and has regained a role in leadership. The bond of Christian love that flows between us helps me deal with an unpleasant memory.

Scriptural Challenge

If two texts indicate opposite views, we must take the challenge to "rightly [explain] the word of truth" (2 Tim 2:15). By exploring every aspect of Scripture we can reconcile the different concepts.

Galatians 6:1 confirms the Christian tradition calling for redemptive love. "Indeed, God did not send the Son into the world to condemn the world, but in order that the world might be saved through him" (John 3:17). Unless we operate the church as a hospital for the spiritually wounded, we miss the purpose of Christ's earthly mission. It is equally as important to lift up the fallen as it is to lead unbelievers to Jesus.

Ideally, we will strive to restore others to wholeness with the same gentle spirit we would want someone to use to correct us. At the same time we recognize our own vulnerability and remember Paul's words of caution: "Take care that you yourselves are not tempted" (Gal 6:1).

The Living Bible paraphrases Galatians 6:1 in a way that may reveal the type of transgression under consideration. "If a Christian is overcome by some sin, you who are godly should gently and humbly help him [or her] back onto the right path." Being *overcome* by sin suggests *unintentional* deviation from following God's will. This kind of transgression warrants greater understanding and compassion than deliberate sin. While the compassion of God is freely available to all, someone who contemplates wrongdoing, considers the consequences, and willingly commits the act may deserve harsher treatment than someone who merely slips up.

To better comprehend the full implications of 1 Corinthians 5:11, we need to examine the circumstances that caused Paul to advise the extreme measure of excommunication. The crime was incest—condemned even by unbelievers then as well as now. Not only did the church fail to discipline the man who was sleeping with his stepmother, members of the congregation prided themselves on their tolerance of deviant behavior.

Acceptance of the homosexual lifestyle today is often seen as equivalent to the incest situation at Corinth. When a practicing homosexual denies the sinful nature of such a lifestyle and professes to be closer to God than ever before, many congregations will disfellowship the person. Shunning the individual is thought to prevent others from being led astray. A majority of church people feel such conduct requires denunciation, not approval.

The injunction against eating with those who flaunt sin perhaps refers to regular meals. If, however, we apply the directive to sharing the Lord's Supper, we symbolically sever the offender from the body of Christ. That prevents corruption that can easily spread.

Actually, the questions raised by two conflicting texts were answered by Jesus when he said, "If another disciple sins, you must rebuke the offender, and if there is repentance, you must forgive" (Luke 17:3). The condition of the heart determines how we should respond.

Whether the sin is intentional or by mistake, we must forgive when repentance occurs. "If the same person sins against you seven times a day, and turns back to you seven times and says, 'I repent,' you

must forgive" (Luke 17:4). God always forgives the contrite heart, and we are required to do likewise.

Restoration of Ministry

Although we must love and accept the fallen leader who truly repents, we might well hesitate to reinstate him or her into a leadership position. The Bible doesn't offer a clear-cut formula for dealing with this issue. Each situation must be worked out to the satisfaction of the leader, those under his or her leadership, and God. Several factors are involved, but the most important is the condition of the heart, which can be judged only by God.

We do have some biblical examples of how God dealt with certain individuals chosen for specific tasks. When God told Moses how to provide water for the Israelites, Moses claimed the honor for himself. His arrogance cost him the privilege of leading the people into the land of Canaan (Num 20:9–13).

While God punished David for the sins of adultery and murder, God did not snatch the throne from the penitent king (2 Sam 12:7–15). David planned and provided materials to build a magnificent temple for the Lord, but God disqualified the warring king from carrying out the mission because of the blood that had been shed at David's command (1 Chron 22:6–8).

After sleeping during the hour when Jesus needed him most and denying his Lord three times, Peter preached a powerful sermon just fifty-three days later.

Although Peter's recovery period was short, it was marked by a dramatic event. The coming of the Holy Spirit filled the impetuous disciple with power to subdue human failure.

Many factors need to be considered when deciding how to respond to a leader's sin. In a situation of that kind, a man I'll call Pastor Martin (not his real name) asked the question: "What would Jesus do?" With that question uppermost in his mind, he worked through the following scenario.

The sin of a person I'll refer to as Leslie (name has been changed) had become public knowledge within the congregation as well as throughout the community. While not holding an official position in the church, Leslie occasionally took a role in worship services.

"In view of all we now know, what parameters would you like to establish regarding Leslie's participation in the church?" Pastor Martin asked the twenty-four-member spiritual arm of the church.

After the group processed available information, a spokesperson said, "We don't have any specific boundaries at this time. We are content with your judgment, Pastor Martin." Since Leslie did not desire an up-front position, the pastor decided to take a cautious approach.

A short time later a serious illness threatened the life of a child in the church. While waiting for a medical report, the parents paced the corridor of the hospital, oblivious to everything happening around them. Suddenly, they both became aware that Leslie was singing a song on the radio. They stopped to listen. In that moment, they perceived that God was sending them a message through Leslie's song. God seemed to be saying, "The child will live."

The child's subsequent recovery called for a celebration with the church family. In planning the service, the parents approached the pastor. "Will it be all right to ask Leslie to sing the song that touched our hearts in the hospital?"

As Pastor Martin briefly hesitated, the question again flashed before his mind: "What would Jesus do?" Christ's treatment of Mary Magdalene provided the answer. Pastor Martin acted on the premise that the potential value to the family outweighed any negative aspects that might result from his affirmative decision.

A distinction should be made between various levels of leadership. We might reinstate an usher or a choir member sooner than a pastor, evangelist, or teacher. Guidelines can be less stringent for persons who perform a service than for spiritual leaders who influence the eternal destiny of souls.

Recovery Period

Quite often the person who has fallen feels the need to take time out for healing. In fact, a pastor or leader who insists on an immediate return to ministry may lack the remorse that properly accompanies repentance. Time heals many things.

Any deviation from a Christian code of conduct indicates neglect for the influence of the Holy Spirit. As the source of our spiritual strength, the Holy Spirit is present to keep us from falling. If we disregard that presence and yield to sin, we need to seek a fresh infilling of the Holy Spirit. Praying with an accountability group during a recovery period will likely be more effective than questing for healing by oneself. Our search may result in a climactic experience, or it may simply produce a strong dedication to faithfulness.

Before we can silence the echoes of yesterday's sins, we may need to make restitution. That could involve financial recompense as it did for Zacchaeus (Luke 19:8). It might require the restoration of a relationship as it did for Onesimus (Philem 8–17). As much as possible we are required to restore what was lost as a consequence of sin.

Sometimes fallen leaders allow remorse to paralyze them from moving beyond regret. Especially if we mess up big time, we have difficulty in forgiving ourselves.

One way to gain victory over guilt that remains after confessing the sin is to fight whatever caused the downfall. For instance, a person freed from addiction to pornography is a good candidate to wage the battle against indecent literature or movies.

While working with the homeless in Portland, my husband, Kurt, met a man who demonstrated the value of helping others bound by a habit that had caused his own personal failure.[1] Timothy was a welcome sight in skid row because the well-dressed man pushed a grocery cart filled with hamburgers. My hungry husband gratefully received two hamburgers, but he was extremely curious about what motivated the generosity.

Hoping to learn more, Kurt said, "Sir, may I go with you?"

"Sure, you can hand these out," Timothy said with a smile.

"To whom?"

"To anybody who comes along."

After handing out all the hamburgers, the benefactor said to Kurt, "Thanks for helping me." Reluctant to leave, Kurt continued to follow along. "Would you like to talk?" Timothy asked.

"Sure," Kurt replied.

They sat on the step of a nearby building and began to get acquainted. After learning about Kurt's mission on the streets, Timothy related his own story.

Once a successful businessman with a beautiful home, a wife, and children, Timothy tried to escape the pressures of work with a few drinks. Soon he became addicted. "Alcohol was the main reason I lost my job, and it was also the reason my family left me," he said.

For six years Timothy had lived on skid row. Then the pastor at a mission told him about Jesus. After receiving new life in Christ, Timothy began the long road to recovery. Starting out as a janitor in a fast-food restaurant, the entrepreneur had become a partner in the business.

"I made a promise to God that if I ever got a chance at success again, I would give some back to the street people. Maybe I could be an encouragement to someone like the pastor was to me," the humble servant of God said. Thus, he passed out hamburgers every other night and provided love and counsel to anyone who wanted another chance at life.

Restoration takes place in God's time. Healing may come swiftly or slowly, but we can hasten the process through our efforts to bring wholeness to others who are broken by the same sins that brought us down.

Reader Challenge

• Does memory of past failure still haunt you? Have you fully yielded yourself to the Holy Spirit? If you are struggling in this area, will you find someone to help you? What action on your part would help erase the consequences of past sin?

• After you have done all you know to do, will you take Philippians 3:13–14 as your motto? "This one thing I do: forgetting what lies behind and straining forward to what lies ahead, I press on toward the goal for the prize of the heavenly call of God in Christ Jesus."

• Do you hold any remnant of resentment for a leader who has disappointed or embarrassed you? Perhaps taking the following steps will help you adjust your attitude. Mental imagery is required for part of the exercise and could be used throughout. The impact will be greater, however, if you literally

go through the process of performing the described activities.

√ To program your mind for better reception, read John 8:1–11. In fact, you might read it three times, focusing on a different protagonist each time—the Pharisees, the woman, and Jesus.

√ When you have finished, picture Jesus standing before you holding two stones. He hands you one and asks you to write on the stone the name of someone you judge harshly. Below the name write the nature of the offense. At first you feel smug in exposing the sin, but under the intense scrutiny of Jesus you begin to squirm with discomfort.

√ Jesus places the second stone beside the first. He says nothing, but you know what you must do. Identifying your own sins is painful, and you fear someone will observe what you confess. You pause as though finished, then you see sadness in the eyes of Jesus. "Unforgiveness," you add.

√ Two stones side by side represent two lives marred by sin. Is there a difference? You want to believe your sin is more justifiable, but you realize that sin is sin.

√ After allowing you a moment to experience the impact of your discovery, Jesus hands you a jar of red paint to symbolize his blood shed for the sins of humankind. Quickly you begin to cover your sins. Before you finish, though, Jesus places his finger over the word, "Unforgiveness."

√ The implication of his action is clear. Picking up the other stone, you completely blot out the writing with the red paint. Then, with a clear conscience, you feel the freedom to clear your own record through the blood of Jesus. Joy floods your soul as your eyes meet the eyes of Jesus and you perceive a surge of love flowing between you and your Savior.

• You are now in a position to pray effectively.

OH, GOD, I am so unworthy of the price you paid for my sins. Thank you for your love and for the forgiveness that is mine as I forgive others. "Now to him who is able to keep [me] from falling, and to make [me] stand without blemish in the presence of his glory with rejoicing, to the only God [my] Savior, through Jesus Christ [my] Lord, be glory, majesty, power, and authority, before all time and now and forever. Amen" (Jude 24—25).

---

1. Salierno, 106–108.

CHAPTER 13

Holding Others Accountable

God speaks to the prophet: "If I say to the wicked, 'You shall surely die,' and you give them no warning ... those persons shall die for their iniquity; but their blood I will require at your hand" (Ezek 3:18).

If that sounds like heavy responsibility, it is. Not only are we as Christian leaders called to personal accountability, we are required to hold others accountable as well. We are not liable for how they respond, but we are required to sound the warning.

No Compromise

If we wish to avoid reaching the judgment bar with blood-stained hands, we will uphold the truths of God's Word without compromise. Under certain circumstances we may hesitate to lay the truth on the line even though we strongly believe it is needed. We don't like to offend people or come across as preachy.

When speaking or teaching in the public arena, we might be tempted to concentrate on safe issues rather than to arouse controversy. We don't like to offend people and run the risk of losing them from the church.

As important as it is to take the message of God's love and grace to the world, we need also to include God's standard of holiness and God's judgment for disobedience. Anything less constitutes deception.

That does not call for harsh preaching or teaching. According to the Apostle Paul, we need to recognize both "the kindness and the severity of God" (Rom 12:22).

In keeping with God's kindness we will want to be as diplomatic as possible when exposing sin. Timing can be important. If we lambaste immorality the first time the scarlet woman enters the church door, she may never return. On the other hand, if she can first be drawn to Jesus through love, she may denounce her sin through the influence of the Holy Spirit.

It is possible for two preachers to preach the same message with opposite objectives. Suppose they both preach that people are going to hell, but one minister seems to enjoy the prospect while the other sincerely regrets that even one person will face eternal damnation. Which one will be more effective for God?

No matter how much love we may express or how much diplomacy we use, such effort will not always get the job done. At times we are required to uphold the biblical standard regardless of the consequences.

Christian leaders who fear public censure may hide behind the excuse that people won't listen anyway. Through a clever analogy, a *Focus on the Family* reader showed the fallacy of that argument. In a letter to the editor, Anthony Ducklow revealed how driver's education would be taught under the same rationale currently applied to sex education.

"Welcome to Driver's Education 101!" a teacher would begin. "I would like to go over some ways for 'safe driving.' While a majority of drivers prefer driving on the right side of the road, some of you may choose to drive on the left side. This is a moral choice, and only you can decide what is right—not your parents or your friends. If you do decide to drive on the left side, use protection. Drive only automobiles that contain airbags. Airbags save lives!

"The same goes for red lights and stop signs. Some will tell you that you should terminate your acceleration at these designated areas. This is another moral choice. I cannot tell you what is right or wrong. You will have to decide whether this particular life choice is for you. But remember, education is key when it comes to safe driving!"[1]

How far would that line of reasoning get with the police or with a judge? Not far, I suggest.

Through my work in schools and universities I have discovered that students like to hear the truth about sexuality. Educators tell me to shift my emphasis from abstinence to safe sex, but God requires me to adhere to Scripture. In response to my message of sexual purity, I have received standing ovations in inner-city schools where the initial reaction of the audience was hostile.

After my challenge to chastity in one university, students streamed down front to pray even though we had no altar in the gymnasium. The demonstration of emotion resembled an old-time revival as young men and women pleaded for God to touch them with the cleansing power of the Holy Spirit.

Wanting to make the most of what was happening, I inquired, "Would anyone like to say something?"

A man who had been praying in so much agony I feared he might be having a heart attack came forward. "I need to apologize to some of the girls I've dated," he said. "You know who you are, and I want to say I'm sorry for what I did to you."

His honesty and brokenness caused others to respond in like manner. Hearts melted as individuals confessed their sins to God and to each other.

Those who contend that biblical standards are outdated do not reckon with the power of the Holy Spirit at work. When individuals yield to the inner voice of the Holy Spirit, life-changing experiences result.

Financial Fallout

Dollar signs sometimes tempt us to remain silent on issues that would offend heavy contributors. If an unscrupulous businessman pledges ten thousand dollars to the building fund, we might hesitate to come on strong regarding the importance of integrity. We might even save the subject for some Sunday when he is absent.

Although I wasn't part of the decision-making process, I became indirectly involved in a situation regarding possible financial fallout. A prominent man had donated large sums of money to a Christian university. Either his son or his daughter who attended the university broke several rules and messed up big-time.

"What do we do?" officials at the university asked. "If we suspend or discipline the student, we might lose the funds."

Because of my connection, I followed the case with interest. When someone asked for my unofficial opinion, I said, "You have to keep up the quality of the school. If you compromise on one student, you're not being fair to the other students. Let the heavy contributor decide what he wants to do about the money."

Ultimately, the decision was made to treat the student the same as anyone else. I don't know if the father withdrew his support, but from all indications the school is surviving quite well.

Some people use money as a means to control church policy. While not as serious as the sin issue, this can pose a problem if the pastoral staff feels God leading in a different direction. As we evaluate individual situations, we need to keep in mind that

God will provide for a program instituted by the Holy Spirit.

Personal Confrontation

Not all responsibility for holding others accountable can be discharged from the pulpit or lectern. If an individual fails to live up to truth preached or taught, our only option is to confront him or her personally.

Early in my ministry I took a staff position to work with a particular segment of the congregation. Prior to my arrival, a volunteer had performed the duties I was to assume. Because I appreciate volunteers, I wanted her to continue serving and hoped the two of us could work together.

The arrangement worked well until I discovered that a couple involved in leadership had adopted an immoral lifestyle. "We need to correct this situation," I said, but my coworker did not see it as a problem. "God will not honor our work if we condone sin," I insisted.

"You're entitled to your opinion, but we're not going to do anything about it."

As a newcomer, I didn't want to challenge an older woman who had been in the church a long time, but I felt I had no choice. "The church hired me to be responsible for this area of ministry," I said. "At this point I'm going to have to do what I think is right."

My stand did not sit well with the woman. When it became obvious I could not amiably resolve the

issue with her, I decided to take the matter to the pastor.

After hearing me out, the pastor said, "I agree with you. Do what you must do, but be careful to handle the truth in love."

Although I tried to project love when I asked the two people to step down, they responded in anger to the truth. God's blessing on the ministry or the welfare of their own souls did not concern them. They wanted only to preserve the illusion that they could get by with sin.

As a consequence of my action, the woman who opposed me left the church. My ministry in that church did not start out as I had hoped at all, and that was painful.

From that point on, however, the ministry took on a deeper quality of spirituality. By setting a standard for leaders, we demonstrated what we wanted God to accomplish in the pew. The Holy Spirit began to generate enthusiasm for Christian living, and outsiders began to seek for the missing ingredient in their own lives.

Denial of Sin

Some people agree that certain behavior constitutes sin, but they deny their own involvement in that sin. Before the sin can be dealt with, such persons must admit they are sinning.

One of my colleagues in ministry has had considerable counseling experience regarding sinful behaviors. His recommendations for bringing secret sin into the open are worth passing on.

First, act only on concrete evidence, not rumor. Suppose someone goes to the pastor or other leader and says, "Did you know that Mr. X is involved in pornography?"

"No, are you sure?"

While the evidence sounds incriminating, Mr. X might have a plausible explanation. When there is room for doubt, the pastor needs to help the accuser recognize the possibility of error.

If the accuser demonstrates genuine concern for the spiritual welfare of Mr. X rather than delight in another's sin, the pastor will want to advise the individual to follow the biblical formula for fostering reconciliation.

With Matthew 18:15–17 in mind, the pastor might say, "Have you talked to Mr. X about this?"

"No, I don't want to do that because it might jeopardize my business relationship with him."

"I'm sorry, but there is nothing I can do until you follow the first step required by Jesus."

That closes the matter for the present. A short while later, however, someone else comes forth with an even stronger charge against Mr. X.

Following the pastor's advice, this person confronts Mr. X, who denies the accusation. In fact, Mr. X refuses to confess wrongdoing even when faced with concrete proof rather than circumstantial evidence.

After two other persons in the congregation present a case against Mr. X, the pastor and the three members meet with the man addicted to pornography. Again, Mr. X denies the charges.

According to Jesus, the matter then goes before the church. This could be handled within a small group such as a leadership council. If he still refuses to be brought to accountability, Mr. X will then be stripped of the privileges of membership in the body of Christ. Because of the nature of the offense, parents will need to be warned of the danger he poses to their children and youth.

To summarize: we need to act only on facts rather than hearsay. The accuser should first approach the accused, and then follow up with witnesses. As a last resort, the matter goes before the church. Until the guilty person confesses the sin, reconciliation cannot take place. Leaders cannot hold people accountable who are unwilling to respond.

The Authoritative Voice

During a counseling session a leader may very well dispense advice on two levels. The more authoritative voice comes from Scripture. Any excuse for violating biblical commands is null and void. When the Bible tells us not to steal, no one can rationalize, "I'm underpaid, so what I take from my employer is rightfully mine."

If we are to hold people accountable, we cannot leave room for negotiation on issues where Scripture clearly speaks. That is not to say that we should give up on people who fail to measure up immediately. We need to work with the person who is struggling to break free from an immoral relationship. Our encouragement may mean the difference between ultimate success and failure.

Along with absolute directives, we also offer advice based on wisdom. Scripture may shed light on the subject without dealing specifically with the issue. For instance, Johnny's parents go to the pastor and say, "What are we going to do about Johnny? He's becoming rebellious."

After asking several questions, the pastor learns that a major battle took place after the parents issued an ultimatum to Johnny regarding his hairstyle. "When teens today must make serious choices with eternal consequences, you might want to take a more relaxed approach regarding hairstyle," the pastor advises.

"Doesn't the Bible say it is a shame for a man to have long hair?" the father asks.

The pastor must agree, but the single reference in 1 Corinthians 11 also requires women to have long hair and wear veils, which not many women observe. Scholars generally believe this instruction related to local customs in Corinth.

Scripture does not firmly support either the view of the parents or the pastor, but wisdom suggests flexibility in dealing with today's teens unless a matter of absolute right and wrong is involved. "Do not provoke your children to anger" (Eph 6:4) strengthens the argument for tolerance. When the Bible provides no clear-cut guidelines on an issue, we must make the best possible judgment by "rightly explaining the word of truth" (2 Tim 2:15).

Staff Requirements

Anyone who falls into sin casts a reflection on the entire congregation. This is especially true when staff members are involved. As a preventive measure, the senior pastor or person in charge might initiate a policy requiring all paid staff members to enter into an accountability relationship with at least one or two persons.

Making a similar demand on volunteers could result in a shortage of workers, but the example set by the staff will encourage others to follow. The concept of accountability might be taught during a teachers' meeting, choir practice, or Christian education committee meeting. If given time to assimilate the idea, workers may be more inclined to participate.

Inappropriate handling of funds shatters the morale within a congregation. To avoid catastrophe, anyone with access to money should be held to strict accountability. If careful scrutiny of financial transactions is presented as a safeguard of integrity rather than distrust of individuals, no one should be offended.

Just as Jesus taught his disciples to pray, "Lead us not into temptation" (Matt 6:13, NIV), we can help preserve the honesty of subordinates by limiting the opportunity for wrongdoing.

Likewise, Christian employers who monitor the transactions of employees contribute to the character of the workers. The following true story illustrates the validity of that observation. Names have been changed.

As wife of the owner, Gloria handled the finances at Northern Tool, a distributor for several manufacturing companies. One day Cliff Lawson, the sales manager, presented her with a credit authorization written up by Al Dudley, the local representative of Catco Tools.

"Gloria, would you write out a check to Al Dudley for $850 to offset this credit?" Gloria's raised eyebrows prompted Cliff to add, "We'll make out okay when we receive the credit."

"Yes, I see how we will make out, but how will Catco Tools make out?"

"Uh ... well, it's rather complicated, and you wouldn't understand it."

"Try me." The dubious explanation that followed caused Gloria to agree. "You're right, I don't understand it. Before I can write a check, I'll need an invoice from Catco Tools."

While Lawson went to get an invoice from Dudley, Gloria debated how she should handle the matter. With the invoice she could question Catco Tools as to whether or not the transaction was legitimate, but she did not want to do that unless absolutely necessary.

An idea formed in her mind as she remembered occasional dealings with another tool representative. When Northern Tool needed tools in a hurry, the representative would pick them up from another distributor. He then requested that Gloria make out a check to him followed by the manufacturer's name.

When Lawson returned with the invoice, Gloria wrote a check to Al Dudley—Catco Tools Company.

A short while later Lawson returned the check. "It won't work," he said.

The two men never again proposed a suspicious deal. Subordinates in the workplace and in the church need to know they will be held accountable to operate with honesty.

Reader Challenge

• In what areas do people under your leadership fail to live up to biblical standards? Have you neglected preaching or teaching on these topics because you fear offending people or losing their financial or emotional support? Will you now commit yourself to deal with these issues regardless of the consequences?

• Is the spiritual climate in your congregation cooled by secret sin? How will you deal with it?

• Write out the themes you have addressed during the past six months of your ministry. Differentiate between the ones that represent biblical instruction and the ones that represent human wisdom. Which ones take top priority?

• What steps have you taken or will you take to protect your subordinates from the evil influence of the world?

• Review Ezekiel 3:18–21 before you pray.

ALMIGHTY GOD, it is an awesome responsibility to hold others accountable—especially when I recognize the shortcomings in my own life. Give me insight to teach truth where it is needed. Help me to support biblical instruction with a holy lifestyle. As I sound heaven's warning, keep me faithful until I join the company of believers to celebrate everlasting life. In Jesus' name, Amen.

---

1. Anthony Ducklow, "Family Mail," *Focus on the the Family,* July 1996: 16.

CHAPTER 14

When Leadership Requires Risk

The pursuit of almost any goal requires a measure of risk. A person starting a business under ideal conditions has no guarantee of success. Sales could slump if a new and improved product hits the market. A competitor may set up shop across the street and offer lower prices. When someone quits a well-paying job to start a new business, he or she risks losing the original investment as well as a secure future.

So why do we take risks? Sometimes the possibility of making it big overcomes our fear of failure. Confidence in our own ability contributes to our willingness to take a bold step. Christian leaders, of course, will place their confidence in God rather than in themselves. If we truly believe God is leading us in a certain direction, our faith will carry us through the rough spots.

In considering this issue, I believe a distinction should be made between a *risk* and a *gamble*. People who buy lottery tickets, play poker, or place bets on a football game often justify their actions with the reasoning, "All of life is a gamble."

Although the two words are sometimes used interchangeably, a gamble usually involves putting up money in the hopes of winning a big prize. The principle is wrong. Either the gambler wastes money or strikes it rich at the expense of others who bet and lose. The desire for instant wealth without earning it hardly represents the Christian philosophy regarding money.

The kind of risk we want to encourage is a faith venture. We should take risks to build up God's kingdom rather than for possible selfish gain.

Big Dreams

The risk factor relates to accountability in that we help each other evaluate our visions and decide which ones promise rewards great enough to warrant stepping out on faith. As my speaking career began to escalate, I asked the women in my core group to brainstorm goals I might pursue.

"I could see Lori speaking at America West Arena," one of the women said.

Everyone laughed—especially me. "Come on, be real," I said. To my mind only major sporting events or performances featuring top recording artists could command an audience in Phoenix's most prestigious entertainment center with a seating capacity of nearly twenty thousand.

"Let's just talk about it," the woman with the idea said. "What would the scene look like?"

"There would probably be a lot of people there," someone said.

"The stage would probably be down on the floor where the basketball players normally are."

"It would be dark with the spotlight on you."

As the women continued to paint a picture, I began to catch a spirit of enthusiasm, but I still thought we were on a trip to fantasy land. "Okay, okay. Will the audience be quiet or rowdy?" I asked.

"They'll be rowdy at first, but they'll settle down when you begin to speak."

"All right, all right," I said, feigning faith I didn't possess.

Four months later I received an invitation to make a fifteen-minute gospel presentation in that arena during a Christian concert. Through an accountability group we can keep each other motivated to do our best. It's hard to settle for the mediocre when others are saying, "Go for the gold. You can do it."

Tough Decisions

Changing careers can be scary business. A wrong move could result in disaster. Especially if we leave a successful career to experience failure, we might lose a position of leadership altogether. Too easily we could slip into a mood of despondency from which we might never recover.

After finishing graduate school, I took a staff position in the church where my husband was youth minister. Because I wanted to take advantage of some speaking opportunities offered to me, I accepted the staff position on a three-quarter-time basis. That allowed me ninety days a year for speaking engagements.

The arrangement worked great for a while. In the church I taught discipleship classes, taught newcomers classes, worked with the seniors, and developed leadership. Between times I jetted here and there speaking in schools and colleges. I had the best of two worlds.

Then invitations to speak began to pour in, requiring me to be gone for most of the ninety free days I had been granted. At the same time my work with the church demanded more of my energy. I began to burn out.

When my agent informed me that speaking opportunities through his contacts were practically exhausted, he suggested I might be ready for an agency with a wider clientele. My husband, Kurt, and I journeyed to Nashville to check out the possibility. Although the agent I interviewed was willing to sign me up on a part-time basis, he encouraged me to consider resigning my staff position to devote all my energy to speaking.

After the interview, Kurt and I agreed I needed to make a choice between two areas of ministry. I had already had enough experience with burnout to realize I couldn't divide my time and give my best to either the church or the speaking circuit.

My heart leaned toward going on the road full-time, but I had to ask some hard questions. What if the opportunities projected by my agent never materialized? Could I make enough money to supplement Kurt's income? Toward what is God directing me? Of course, God's direction was most important, but many factors must be considered when trying to determine the nature of divine leadership.

As I do in making any decision, I leaned on my husband. At the time, I had not yet established my accountability group with the women. Kurt would need to make the greater sacrifice if I went on the road, but he came through in his usual supportive style.

"Not many people get these kinds of opportunities," Kurt said. "They won't always be there for you. When you're fifty or sixty, students will turn to younger role models. If you ever want this kind of experience, now is the time."

"Here's the thing, Kurt. I don't want to look back fifteen or twenty years from now and say, 'I wonder what would have happened if....' I love being on staff in the local church, but at this time I think I'd like to take advantage of the open door in youth ministry."

The financial insecurity of relying on speaking engagements still concerned me when I discussed resigning with my boss, the senior pastor. "I hope I'm not making a mistake," I said.

I'll forever be grateful to the pastor for his wisdom and sensitivity. "Lori," he said, "let's say you try it for a year. At the end of the year you may decide it was a great experience but you're tired of traveling and don't want to do it anymore. You have an open door here."

"Are you serious?"

"It would have to go through the church, but the people love you. They'll take you back."

I didn't want to use the church as a safety net, but it was much easier to step out on faith, knowing I had that kind of support.

Forerunner in Faith

If making a decision to chart an uncertain future was difficult for me, what must it have been like for Abraham? The man who still inspires Christians to trust in God took more risks than could ever be required of me. In almost every aspect the parallel between his journey of faith and mine is one of contrasts rather than similarities.

Growing up in a pastor's home, I had observed God's track record in honoring faith. God always came through for my parents and others in the church. I had been taught biblical promises even as I learned to walk and talk. Without a role model Abraham had to find his own way. He had to discern the voice of the one true God from among the heathen gods. Instead of receiving benefit from the past experiences of others, Abraham had to make history.

My family and friends support me in my decisions. No doubt Abraham encountered resistance from his peers. "Are you out of your mind, Abe?" friends probably said. "How dare you forsake family responsibility to chase after the whim of a god you have manufactured in your head!" family members likely said.

Modern conveniences create a vast discrepancy between my situation and that of Abraham. After locating my desired destination on a map, I need only book a flight with United Airlines and fly the friendly skies. To reach an undisclosed destination, Abraham and his company tromped through the desert with sand blowing in their faces. Camels, donkeys, sheep, and goats served as their only all-terrain vehicles.

The Lord had already brought Abraham through many perilous circumstances before putting the patriarch to the extreme test. Perhaps past dealings with God enabled Abraham to place his son on the altar and lift the knife to slash the throat of the terrified child of promise. Certainly God's intervention in sparing Isaac's life taught future generations that it's safe to take a risk for God.

Reckless Risks

Regardless of the strong case for risk taking in ministry, we need to exercise caution before undertaking a venture with an uncertain outcome. Risk taking that accomplishes a purpose attests to the value of faith, but a failed venture hinders personal faith and sends a negative message to others. So—how do we know when to move ahead and when to back off?

First, we need to be sure that what we hope to accomplish is backed by God. "Unless the Lord builds the house, those who build it labor in vain" (Ps 127:1). The importance of an alliance with God is obvious, but how do we determine God's position? Doesn't God sanction all efforts to build the kingdom of heaven?

Certainly any program designed to lead individuals to Jesus Christ as Savior concurs with God's agenda. Sometimes, though, personal ambitions cloud the divine purpose. The focus shifts from glorifying God to building a shrine to self.

For instance, a pastor might try to persuade a reluctant board to launch a building program. In response to the argument that the congregation can't afford to expand, the pastor could suggest taking a leap of faith. Such faith may be warranted if the goal truly is to reach lost souls for the Lord. In that case, the pastor will need to inspire others with a vision. This can best be done through prayer and gentle persuasion.

On the other hand, if the pastor uses evangelism to mask a desire to seek a prominent position among peers in ministry, God may not wish to participate in the endeavor. A program that goes forth without God's backing may result in disaster for the congregation as well as for the pastor.

In taking financial risks we need to safeguard against misuse of money in the church treasury. Without consent of the donors, money donated for a particular purpose should not be transferred to another cause regardless of how worthy it might be. While faith allows us to anticipate miracles, fiscal responsibility requires us to make the kind of commitments we will be able to honor. Default of obligations is counterproductive to God's cause.

In these areas we once again see the value of accountability. If we recognize the human tendency to stroke our own egos, we can better evaluate our motives through a frank discussion with those we have chosen to help guide our ministry.

Required Risks

To preserve the reputation of the church or personal integrity, we may need to take risks that make us uncomfortable. We will not always have the opportunity to consider the consequences before stepping out on faith.

For instance, a church rented a house for its new pastor and his family. The landlord stipulated in the agreement that the house should be vacated as soon as his son came home from military service.

Some time later, the minister received notice to move. "Don't worry," members of the board said, "they can't legally throw you out for six months."

In two sentences the pastor preached one of his most powerful sermons. "I don't care if I have to move my family into a tent," he said. "This church will not go back on its word." Obviously, this pastor risked the inconvenience of having to find a new place to live in order to help the congregational leaders keep their agreement with the landlord.

Integrity sometimes leads us to risk financial security. When John McCusker took a job with a telemarketing firm in Phoenix, he believed the company would deliver on promises made to clients. After noting that company policy focused on selling dreams rather than on making dreams come true, McCusker began to suspect the ethics of the principals.

"When will these investments begin to pay off?" he asked.

"Never mind that part. You just keep on selling them," he was told.

Soon McCusker realized the company was based on flagrant fraud. His conscience would not allow him to continue making false claims to potential investors. At a time when his family was already in crisis, McCusker quit his job. With no money, he had to ask himself some hard questions: "Will we be out on the street?" "Will my children go hungry?"

In spite of considerable hardship in the months ahead, the family did not starve or end up homeless. Eventually, God honored McCusker's faith by opening up a position with a Christian organization that provided him an opportunity to develop leadership skills he didn't know he had.

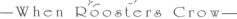

"I think I'll make it now, and I give God the credit," McCusker testified. "Because of the witness of the Holy Spirit, my future looks good, and I held on to my integrity in the past."

If a matter of principle is at stake, we can be sure God is on our side even if hope seems dim. That does not mean we will always be spared from adversity. The Apostle Paul listed in his second letter to the Corinthians adversities he had suffered as a result of risking for the Lord (chapter 11). His conclusion was that God's grace was sufficient for him (2 Cor 12:9), no matter what he faced.

Reader Challenge

• What would you aspire to accomplish for the Lord if you did not fear failure? What risks are involved?

• When I think a goal is beyond my reach, I remember a statement once made by my pastor: "If your dream is small enough for you to handle, it isn't big enough for God." Meditate on that thought for a moment. How does it change your perspective?

• Write out what you might do to take your ministry one step beyond what it is today. Will you make this your goal? Who will help you keep focused on your goal? Who will encourage you when you are about to give up?

• Could any of the risks you contemplate taking for God actually be based on your personal ambitions? If you have any doubts about your motives, will you find someone to help you honestly evaluate your goals?

• Does anything in your lifestyle compromise Christian principles? If so, will you risk making whatever change is necessary? Remember, risk backed by God is safer than security based on human ability.

• How can you adjust the following prayer to make it your own?

GOD, when I think of what you risked in sending your Son to die for me, any risk I must take pales in comparison. Thank you, God, for taking a chance on me. Help me to disregard my fears when I need to step out on faith for you. Give me the courage to move ahead or the patience to wait for the Holy Spirit's leadership. Give me the wisdom to know which direction to take. In Jesus' name I pray. Amen.